Turning Psychology into a Social Science

This radical book explores a new understanding of psychology based on human engagement with external contexts, rather than what goes on inside our heads. It is part of a trilogy that offers a new way of doing psychology, focusing on people's social and societal environments as determining their behaviour, rather than internal and individualistic attributions.

By showing that we engage directly with our complex social, political, economic, patriarchal, colonized, and cultural contexts and that what we do and think arises from this direct engagement with these external contexts, Bernard Guerin expertly demonstrates that Western ideas have systematically excluded the 'social' but that this is really where the major determinants of our behaviour arise. This book works through many human activities that psychology still treats as individualized and internal and shows their social and societal origins. These includes beliefs, the sense of self, the arts, religious behaviours, and the new and growing area of conservation psychology. The social structures found by sociology, anthropology, and sociolinguistics are shown to shape most 'individual' human actions, and it is shown how the main points of Marxism and Indigenous knowledges can be better merged into this new and broader social science.

Replacing the 'internal' attributions of causes with external contextual analyses based in the social sciences, this book is fascinating reading for academics and students in psychology and the social sciences, and provides exciting new ways to conceptualize and observe human actions in new ways and to resist the current individualistic thinking of 'psychology'.

Bernard Guerin has worked in both Australia and New Zealand researching and teaching to merge psychology with the social sciences. His main research now focuses on contextualizing 'mental health' behaviours, working with Indigenous communities, and exploring social contextual analyses especially for language use and thinking.

Exploring the environmental and social foundations of human behaviour

Series editor
Bernard Guerin
Professor of Psychology, University of South Australia

Can you imagine that everything people do, say, and think is shaped directly by engaging with our many environmental and social contexts? Humans would then really be part of their environment.

For current psychology, however, people only engage with metaphorical 'internal' environments or brain events, and everything we do somehow originates hidden in there. But what if all that we do and think originated out in our worlds, and what we call 'internal' is merely language and conversations that were also shaped by engaging in our external discursive, cultural, and societal environments?

Exploring the Environmental and Social Foundations of Human Behaviour is an exciting new book series about developing the next generation of ways to understand what people do, say, and think. Human behaviour is shaped through directly engaging in our diverse contexts of resources, social relationships, economics, culture, discourses, colonization, patriarchy, society, and the opportunities afforded by our birth contexts. Even language and thinking arise from our external social and discursive contexts, and so the 'internal' and brain metaphors will disappear as psychology becomes merged with the social sciences.

The series is therefore a-disciplinary and presents analyses or contextually engaged research on topics that describe or demonstrate how human behaviour arises from direct engagement with the worlds in which we are embedded.

In this series:

How to Rethink Mental Illness*: The Human Contexts Behind the Labels: Volume 1*

How to Rethink Human Behavior*: A Practical Guide to Social Contextual Analysis: Volume 2*

How to Rethink Psychology*: New Metaphors for Understanding People and Their Behavior: Volume 3*

Turning Psychology into Social Contextual Analysis*: Volume 4*

Turning Psychology into a Social Science*: Volume 5*

Turning Mental Health into Social Action*: Volume 6*

Turning Psychology into a Social Science

Bernard Guerin

LONDON AND NEW YORK

First published 2021
by Routledge
2 Park Square, Milton Park, Abingdon, Oxon OX14 4RN

and by Routledge
52 Vanderbilt Avenue, New York, NY 10017

Routledge is an imprint of the Taylor & Francis Group, an informa business

© 2021 Bernard Guerin

The right of Bernard Guerin to be identified as author of this work has been asserted by him in accordance with sections 77 and 78 of the Copyright, Designs and Patents Act 1988.

All rights reserved. No part of this book may be reprinted or reproduced or utilised in any form or by any electronic, mechanical, or other means, now known or hereafter invented, including photocopying and recording, or in any information storage or retrieval system, without permission in writing from the publishers.

Trademark notice: Product or corporate names may be trademarks or registered trademarks, and are used only for identification and explanation without intent to infringe.

British Library Cataloguing-in-Publication Data
A catalogue record for this book is available from the British Library

Library of Congress Cataloging-in-Publication Data
A catalog record has been requested for this book

ISBN: 978-0-367-89813-7 (hbk)
ISBN: 978-0-367-89812-0 (pbk)
ISBN: 978-1-003-02127-8 (ebk)

Typeset in Times
by Newgen Publishing UK

Contents

List of tables vi
Preface vii
Acknowledgements ix
A note on referencing x

1 The opposite of rational is social, not irrational or crazy: how the 'social' got squeezed out of Western history 1

2 How are our behaviours shaped by societal 'systems' and 'structures'? 35

3 The societal ecologies of modern life *are* our 'psychology' 48

4 Contextualizing beliefs as everyday language strategies 76

5 Self, identity, consciousness, and meaning as social actions in context 89

6 A new look at Marxism, psychology, and social contextual analysis 104

7 Contextualizing the arts 119

8 Contextualizing religion and religious behaviours 127

9 Weaning yourself off social psychology 143

Index 166

Tables

1.1	Nine domains of knowledge that have excluded the 'social', with examples of discourses of the 'rational' and the 'irrational', and how the 'social' should be highlighted	12
1.2	Properties of different forms of social relationships and how these are mirrored in our relationship with the natural environment	27
3.1	Social properties found in three different types of social relationship	62
3.2	Social properties of capitalism and behaviours that are shaped when living in capitalism	68
3.3	Social properties of bureaucracies and some behaviours that are shaped when living in capitalism	70
9.1	Different research methodologies contextualized as social relationships	155
9.2	Six 'phenomena' from social psychology and how they differ only because they use different manipulations of social consequences and different measurements	163

Preface

As I hope the reader will discover, this series of books is not about providing a new theory of psychology, and especially not a 'grand theory', even though the contents might suggest that. It is also not providing a new philosophy, except in a broad sense not related to Western philosophy.

The approach argues, in fact, that words do not have 'meaning' nor do they represent, refer to, or express anything and that argues against the whole Western tradition of philosophy. The only thing words do is to change the behaviour of other people *given the right social contexts*. And that is all this huge collection of words is trying to do.

Most of my words that follow are therefore trying to get you, the reader, to observe the world in new ways; be sensitized to see things you did not see before, and then act in new ways on that basis where appropriate. Most of current psychology, I argue, is just looking in the wrong places for answers and explanations. Because they do not find the answers there, they invent even more abstract words and use correlations to support them, so it looks as if we have discovered something.

The first book in this new trilogy goes back to before the 'cognitive revolution' and shows that the whole reasoning for even having a revolution was mistaken. Psychology took a wrong turn by the assumption that humans must 'go beyond the information given'. Instead, I show how all the subsequent ideas of 'processing information' and 'internal constructions and representations' were really about the social uses of language, and all these ideas and theories can be replaced when we 'turn psychology inside out'. Language use is shown to be externally driven by properly observing all social and societal contexts and realizing that thinking is just language use not said out loud. I then show how we can replace our 'psychology' with the diverse life contexts in which we are immersed, and explore how we can contextualize perception, emotion, and thinking in this way so they do not originate 'inside our heads'.

This second book in this new trilogy shows how the other social sciences have already explored our life contexts, and once we are rid of the current abstract explanations in terms of an 'internal' world, we can merge 'psychology' into the social sciences to form a rich analysis of how humans adapt and become attuned to all of our life contexts. In particular, I explore how our behaviours are now hugely shaped by the modern worlds of capitalism, neoliberalism, and bureaucracy, and how the Marxist frameworks are incompatible with current psychology but can be merged in a contextual approach. Several of the very 'individualistic' ideas embedded in current psychology are then shown to arise directly from our complex social, cultural, and societal worlds, and not from 'inside' us. In particular, I turn the 'psychology' of beliefs, the self, the arts, religious behaviours, and many of the 'individual' phenomena of social psychology inside out, to show their external contexts of origin.

The third book in this new trilogy applies social contextual analysis to the important area of 'mental health'. The behaviours observed in 'mental health' issues are treated here as ordinary behaviours that have been shaped in very bad life situations to become exaggerated and trapped because alternative solutions are blocked. To support the many current attempts to stop using the *Diagnostic and Statistical Manual of Mental Disorders* (DSM), I explore all the individual DSM-listed behaviours and show how they can be shaped by living in bad situations with no alternatives, and are not the result of any brain 'disorders'. The types of bad life situations are explored further, and it is shown that many other behaviours are shaped in addition to the 'mental health' behaviours: violence, bullying, escape, alternative lifestyles, self-harm, exploitation of other people, crime, drug taking. It is suggested that all those people involved in any of these outcomes from bad life situations, professionals, and first-hand experiencers, should pool their expertise and integrate how we can *fix their bad life situations rather than try and fix the person*. Based on these conclusions, interventions for fixing bad life situations are explored, including fixing local issues, fixing those bad social situations that interfere with language use and thinking, and how we might begin to tackle those bad situations produced by our current societal contexts and that are leading to new 'mental health' behaviours: capitalism, neoliberalism, bureaucracy, stratifications, colonization, and patriarchy.

Acknowledgements

The books in this series are a culmination of over 45 years of thinking and researching about these issues, taking every approach seriously, and learning from all of psychology and the social sciences (especially sociology, social anthropology, and sociolinguistics). There are too many people to thank (or even remember) from whom I have learned, so I want to really thank again everyone I have acknowledged in my previous books. You know who you are, I hope. All my students from all my courses have also helped shape my writing when I have used them to try out new ideas and analyses—many thanks.

I also want to thank the staff at Routledge for their belief in this trilogy (and the previous one) and their excellent editing and production work.

A note on referencing

First, each book of the series of six is self-contained, and I have aimed to make them readable alone. However, for those brave souls attempting to see the bigger picture, I use cross-referencing of volume number and chapter in this way: V4.7 refers to Chapter 7 of Volume 4 in the series.

Second, I wish to say upfront that this book comes from reading the work of many researchers and authors across all of psychology and all of the social sciences over many years. In my earlier books I have given hundreds of references to the work of others that has shaped my thinking, even when I disagree. However, I know that referencing slows down a lot of readers whom I would like to take something away from these books that might be of use to them. Many of my intended readers also do not have the privilege of being able to track down the references in any case.

For these reasons, I am being a very bad academic in these books and mostly refer to my own summary works. This current book has been intentionally written so that it can be understood without knowing those earlier books, but to academics (real ones, not me) this causes distress because it looks like I am claiming others' ideas when I use a lot of self-referencing. I certainly do not intend this but having thousands of references interrupting the text causes distress to other readers. This time, I am balancing the distress the other way. You can find the references in my earlier books if needed.

Obviously, where I use or rely heavily on someone's work I cite it and academics can look up all the references if they like and find the sources.

Please do not assume that because I make broad claims and then only cite an earlier summary of my own, that I originated all those ideas and claims. I did not. I am bringing all these ideas from many disciplines together so we can get a new picture of humans and what they do, say, and think. I do not want to interrupt the text by hundreds of references, but please do not get the idea that I believe that I originated everything here.

In fact, the entire theme of this and the other books in the series is that everything we do, say, or think originates in our worlds—our social, societal, cultural, discursive, economic, colonized, patriarchal, and stratified worlds. And that includes my writing these books!

1 The opposite of rational is social, not irrational or crazy
How the 'social' got squeezed out of Western history

One of our main ways of changing other people's behaviour is to use language to convince them. This might be to convince them about social relationships ("I'm so glad to have a friend like you!") or about the world ("If we cannot slow the rate of global warming, all life will die out by the end of this century!"). We can convince people in many different ways (Guerin, 2003, 2016a) but the two broad strategies are to convince by *naming* consequences:

1. *Using* the consequences of our social relationships ("I would love it if you helped me", "Please don't let me find out that you did not help").
2. *Using* the consequences of the world ("Helping people improves your health", "If you help people then good things will happen to you").

The aim of this chapter is to show that the history of Western 'civilization' has been to get rid of (1) and only use (2). Doing this has been really good for science and understanding the non-social environment, but a disaster for anything and everything to do with understanding human behaviour. It has stopped psychology from being a social science since it has tried, in pretending to be a good 'science', to purge the 'social'.

Some background

A few centuries ago, one form of language use to persuade people became predominant in many areas of Western life—*rational argument* or *logic*. It is not that people could not use this before, but it had been mixed in with other ways to convince people as well—primarily through being in social relationships. The *Dialogues of Plato* from ancient Greece, for example, are a mixture of logical and rational argument with some persuasion through utilizing social relationships—sometimes put together into the term 'rhetoric' or a *competitive* social form of persuasion called 'dialectic' (using yes/no questions; see Ryle, 1971).

Socrates (in Plato) typically used *social* methods of persuasion, including competition and bullying, to get acceptance of his *premises*, and then used *logic* on these premises to force a conclusion. We will see later that getting the premises accepted is the major hurdle and the downfall in logic, so Socrates did this through any form of persuasion he could (see Chapter 7). It is a soft form of verbal bullying to get agreement on weak and vague premises that then, through 'pure logic', reach a conclusion the listener *must* agree with socially. So pure logic, rhetoric, and the dialectical methods of persuasion were mixed in together (Ryle, 1971). Box 1.1 gives some idea of this. Try and follow this through *as a social interaction* (or discourse analysis) rather than as an interplay of ideas (in fact, there is little 'interplay').

Box 1.1 The Socratic form of discourse

Socrates: In this way: He says, does he not? "That which appears to each person really is to him to whom it appears."

Theodorus: Yes, that is what he says.

Socrates: Well then, Protagoras, we also utter the opinions of a man, or rather, of all men, and we say that there is no one who does not think himself wiser than others in some respects and others wiser than himself in other respects; for instance, in times of greatest danger, when people are distressed in war or by diseases or at sea, they regard their commanders as gods and expect them to be their saviours, though they excel them in nothing except knowledge. And all the world of men is, I dare say, full of people seeking teachers and rulers for themselves and the animals and for human activities, and, on the other hand, of people who consider themselves qualified to teach and qualified to rule. And in all these instances we must say that men themselves believe that wisdom and ignorance exist in the world of men, must we not?

Theodorus: Yes, we must.

Socrates: And therefore they think that wisdom is true thinking and ignorance false opinion, do they not?

Theodorus: Of course.

(Plato, 1997, p. 527)

The differences between logic and rationality on the one hand, and social persuasion such as rhetoric or using social consequences on the other, are important to understand, even though they are mixed in real life except for the 'civilized' cases we will see in what follows (Guerin, 2016a).

All talk works (or not) because of the social relationships and what people do, but these outcomes can eventually arise from the world itself (the aim of pure rationality) or from our social relationship patterns (social persuasion) and either can be used for persuasion and belief, and also mixed up.

I can persuade you because of what the world will do for you (at least that which my talk suggests) or because of what our social relationship will do. For example: *suppose I wanted to get you to buy me some bread from the store.*

- *Rationality*: if you buy me some bread I will give you the money and give you $5 extra. If you buy me bread you can walk to the store and get some exercise. If you buy me bread I will give you money and you can have half the bread as well.
- *Social 1*: if you buy me some bread I will be so thankful to you. If you buy me some bread I will tell your mother how wonderful you have been. If you buy me some bread I will repay you another day for your kindness.
- *Social 2*: if you don't buy me some bread I will be so mad at you. If you don't buy me some bread I will tell your mother how nasty you have been. If you don't buy me some bread I will never do anything for you ever again.
- *Rhetoric*: could you please do me a favour and buy me some bread. I would absolutely love it if you went out of your way and bought me some bread, any sort will do, and you would be my hero. I know you believe in kindness and you are a loving and caring person, so would you please, please, pretty please buy me some bread?
- *Ancient dialectic* (also see Chapter 7): it is good to help others, right? ("Yes"). And helping others is also good for the one being helpful, is it not? ("Yes"). And would it be good for someone if their friend did not help them? ("No, of course not"). So, would you help me and buy some bread at the store? ("Errr ...")

Notice the differences between these, even though the two social rationales and the rhetoric are mixed up and complex (as is the use of money that is treated as non-social when it is not). Rationality is based on *stating outcomes for the listener from the non-social world*—what is in it for them, what are the immediate consequences *from the world* for the recipient (promised). The others are actually also about *stating or hinting at* the consequences,

4 The opposite of rational is social

but *those consequences are now social outcomes for the recipient—social relationship consequences* not connected to the bread itself (V4.7). If they get the bread then there is nothing in this act itself that is good for them from the world itself, but there are social events (usually afterwards), or a lack of socially punishing events for Social 2, that are the consequences, but they come from the speaker not the bread itself.

This might seem trivial, but it is a huge problem. Getting rid of using social outcomes in life (see Table 1.1) either *results* in a weakening of our life social relationships or else it directly *causes* this weakening! And because it is all presented in language, it is *all* actually social anyway and so the 'social' will always *seep* into the purely 'rational' events anyway (V4.3).

We can also see the same for *getting someone to believe or agree with something we say* (see Chapter 4):

- *Rationality*: cats are better pets than dogs because you do not have to clean as much. Cats are better pets than dogs because they make less noise. You have to walk dogs a lot.
- *Social 1*: I would love it if you were like me and thought that cats are better pets than dogs. If we could agree that cats are better pets than dogs everything would be so harmonious between us.
- *Social 2*: I am sure we can agree that cats are better pets than dogs, since I have always kept cats and love them. I would hate to think that you preferred dogs to cats. I cannot abide people who do not think that cats are better pets than dogs.
- *Rhetoric*: surely no one but an idiot could imagine that cats are not better pets than dogs. If there is one thing I want you to get right in your tiny brain, it is that cats are better pets than dogs.
- *Dialectic*: it is not good to spend your time cleaning up someone else's mess, right? ("No, of course not"). And keeping a peaceful and quiet home is also good for everyone, is it not? ("Yes"). And so, if you had a choice between something both noisy and messy and something both quiet and clean, the latter would be preferable, would it not? ("Yes, clearly"). So, it would be preferable to have a cat over a dog, would it not follow? ("Absolutely! I'm off now to the animal rescue shelter to get a cat").

This lecturing is not to teach you about the complexities of analysing conversations and discourses (Guerin, 2016a), but to get across one main point, with which you can hopefully agree after all I have just said; that there are differences between 'rational' uses of languages and social uses (see what I did there in that sentence?).

This is not a clear or strong division, certainly not in real life, but it tries to make a distinction between how we use language that *describes* either non-social or social consequences for the listener (whether this is to get them to do or believe something). The fact that the distinction is not very good or clear will actually become important. I will come back to this later, since we will find a constant *slippage* or *seepage* between the two when Western rationality attempts to exclude the social. And given that language only has effects no matter what because of social relationships and their consequences, the social is *always* going to leak into any *discourses* that try to exclude it, unless we get rid of language altogether (Zen, praxis, just doing things; V4.7).

People could certainly use reasoning and logic prior to their huge rise, but what happened during the (so-called, ironically) Enlightenment was that social forms of persuasion and getting people to do things became *actively excluded* from many discourses, leaving rationality as the dominant or sometimes exclusive discourse (Foucault, 1970). Rationality and logic were available prior to this, but they became more prevalent; not because people began believing in their superiority initially, but because other forms were excluded as social relationships in society changed.

Why was the 'social' excluded?

It is difficult to bring together all the possible historical reasons why reason and logic became predominant (cf. Foucault, 1970; Siedentop, 2014). Most accounts outline how logic and rationality became important, but less is given about why the 'social' forms were excluded. Here are five ideas. First, during this period 'scientists' became more actively engaged, and were very successful, in observing and intervening *on the environment* to see what happens—what were the consequences *from the world* when they physically experimented? They made important gains from intervening on the environment, so their language, therefore, obviously changed to be about describing what the world did without worrying about the social consequences of that language. "This is 5cm long" rather than "I will say that this is 5cm long because I like you" or "This is obviously 5cm long to anyone with brains!" This rigidity, as we will see, is usually *good* for science (with some exceptions given in what follows), but the language strategy of only describing salient non-social environmental outcomes was taken over by other areas for social and societal control purposes.

Second, most social scientists also believe that the rise of rationality and logic came about *or was accelerated by* the rise of capitalism and the widespread use of money and national currencies. Money (or capital, more exactly) was seen as separate from the social world, just like planets, trees, or minerals found in the ground. Money seemed to be a new *non-social* part of our environment that needed to be clearly and exactly described *without social influence*, just as science was correctly doing in its research. Economic textbooks describe money as if it was something we found in nature and was independent of humans. However, money is certainly *not* non-social, but it seemed to be and was made to look that way (Guerin, 2016a). Some sociologists and others, perhaps starting with Georg Simmel (1907/1978), believe that capitalism actually 'caused' the use of rational and logical ways of persuading people more directly.

A third reason that rationality and logic probably became more prevalent and other forms less so was because the increase in capitalism forced a reduction in family and community size, and gave rise to an extraordinarily rapid increase in the number of daily 'stranger relationships' for the first time in human history. That is, there was a dramatic increase in everyday relationships between people who had the following properties: they did not really know each other, they did not know each other's families or history, they had little accountability within each other's families, and they most frequently had only a small number of resource ties or interdependencies with each other even if they were important ones. Sociologists have long referred to this as the rise of *contractual relationships*—what I call *stranger relationships*—because these relationships have a contract (usually involving money) at their heart.

The important point for here is that under capitalism, the resource ties with strangers soon became more important than anything people could gain from their families. Social influence became less important than contractual influence because that was where most of the relationships were, and certainly the ones most important for getting resources—even if family relationships were still treated as more important in 'sentimental' ways. Some other properties of this are outlined elsewhere (Guerin, 2016a; see also Chapter 3), but here it is stressed that this also led to a compartmentalization of life; that is, our lives are broken into relationships that do not on the whole interact with each other, bits of our lives can be separated, and contractual relationships dominate most of those compartments.

Now, the point of this modern increase in stranger relationships for rationality was that the use of social forms for convincing people to do or believe things became more difficult when there were no longer strong interconnections between people other than money, as there had been previously for extended families and communities, and especially when the different stranger contacts for any one person also did not interact otherwise with each other. There were less chances to use social forms of convincing if you did not know other people in the recipient's family or networks, since you knew little of the dynamics, history, or strategies of the people and hence could not utilize these in persuasion. Money became the prime resource for sustaining talk in order to have successful effects.

A fourth reason for rationality was because the population of major cities had hugely increased. If one is to use *social forms* of convincing and persuading people to do things, these become less practical over large groups, especially when capitalism had changed the major form of relationships into stranger or contractual relationships with no other (non-contractual) obligations between people (Guerin, 1995, 2016a). Successful use of social persuasion requires knowledge of the people being convinced, their family and background, and their likes and salient consequences. However, the abstractness of rationality and logic meant that these strategies still *could* be used to convince larger numbers of people, and so they became useful for governing or controlling larger populations than ever previously known in human history, not just for science.

For example, if I talk to a friend or to family members and say, "You should help your mother more, because she was upset and complaining when I talked to her yesterday, and you know her back is giving her pain", then this might be influential because it is directly pertinent to our real family relationships, and because we all know each other and find things out so there will be real social outcomes. But if I was to say the same sentence to a group of a thousand strangers, it would not work so well. To do a good job with large groups of people we require more *abstraction* and *generalization* in the *reasons* we give: "Everyone loves their mother. This is basic to all good people. And our mothers need help as they get older. Therefore, please, everyone here, go home and help your mother more." (Perhaps in ancient Greece and Rome, addressing larger groups of non-kin in oratories for the first time led to the rise of political speeches full of logic and rational persuasion; see Bloch, 1975; Brown, 1992; Siedentop, 2014.)

A final reason for the rise of rationality has to do with the uses made of it, its misappropriation, but this is a bit more complex. Rationality (attending only to non-social outcomes) is perfect for science, which only studies the things that *the world does*, such as chemical reactions and planets orbiting the sun, but it is less useful for understanding what people talk about or do.

I do not want to go far into the philosophy of this (V4.3), but the physical effects of dropping a glass vase are very different to the effects of someone *saying*, "That glass will break if you drop it". Both effects can be described in scientific 'rational' language, but they are very different. The first effect has to do with force, acceleration under gravity, and the strength of molecular bonds, roughly, and the 'truth' is in *doing* and *observation*, whether you then talk about it or not. We can watch the glass smash into little pieces if we wish, and we cannot put it back together. The second effect (talking) has to do only with what people (listeners usually) do when someone says, "That glass will break if you drop it" (Guerin, 2016b). Those are the only effects, and they are social only, since *nothing actually happens* to the glass vase when we talk, whereas dropping the glass vase produces very real and observable consequences. In the reality of it all, saying that sentence does also have very real and potentially observable consequences, but they are social consequences (what your talk does to the listener), and they are usually difficult to observe because of the complexities and intricacies of social behaviour and reciprocities. As mentioned before (V1.5, V4.3), words do not have properties of truth or falsity with respect to the non-social world. Saying "That glass will break if you drop it" is neither true nor false with respect to events of the world and the vase; all it does is to change someone's behaviour if the contexts are there (social reciprocities).

As we will see, this applies to 'science talk' as well. There is a huge difference being between *science doing things* in the world and observing, and *science talking* about what has been done and seen. 'Science talking' is also neither true nor false, but what the listener does next *is* real. But from the exclusion of the social, science *statements* come to appear as if they could 'house' truth and falsity, when they do not—only doing can be true or false (or better, happen or not).

But we are given the impression that there is somehow a direct connection between doing science and the words used by science. The science words pretend to be direct descriptions of world events but are actually just ways of affecting people to do things in certain ways. But this meant historically that *everyone* wanted the 'power' of 'being a science' so that *their language use would appear powerful, certain, and authoritative* when in fact it never was. This has also been the history of psychology.

Enough of the philosophy already, but there are two ways this gap (V4.7) has been used over history to control and govern people. First, the rational environmental effects (doing things) are more observable and certain, and come with a lot of authority. You can make all sorts of criticisms and denials to my spoken sentence about the vase earlier, but it is more difficult to disguise or deny the smashed glass vase lying in shards all over the floor.

So, the more we can make our control over people and resources *look like* or *resemble* purely rational or scientific outcomes, the stronger will be that control—even if it is actually just garbage we are saying to control them. We will see this in what follows when money, laws, and bureaucratic rules, which are all really constructed within social relationships (Social 1 and Social 2), are made *to look like* something originating purely from (non-social) environmental outcomes and therefore not contestable (Rationality). Money is made in economic textbooks to *look like* it has non-social environmental origins; it does have effects, but only through people. My cat is not interested in money.

The second use of this difference between social and non-social outcomes for social control over people and resources has occurred when speakers have tried to deny what is otherwise a clearly observable outcome from the environment. Many examples of this, some given in what follows, *are done for perfectly useful and good social reasons* but they are still just talking, and the outcomes are not in the (non-social) environment. There are many examples in which religious groups have ritually given a (probably wrong) version of the world but *doing this ritual is about keeping the community together, not about accurate and scientific reporting*, and that really is important and useful—even if the science is bad. This also occurs when bureaucrats use rules to deny that some world event is occurring (one thinks of Kafka), when people lie or deceive, and when people control others through any sort of promise. And of course, every fledging Western philosopher has grappled with the Platonic questions such as, "If I can talk about a pink unicorn then in some sense pink unicorns must be real!"

We will come to examples of all these points below and in the following chapters. Where doing this is harmless or has a useful social or community outcome, I am not too worried (say when some traditional African laws were based on *both* what truthfully happened and on what the effects on the community will be with different verdicts). But where doing this type of control using rationality and pseudo rationality hurts people, the environment, animals, or plants, then we need to call them out and change them. In either case, the two are certainly not mutually exclusive, and, indeed, as I have just pointed out (see also Guerin, 2016b), socialness is merely a special case of rationality but with difficult-to-see social-environment outcomes.

Labelling the 'non-rational'

Whatever the mixture of reasons, rational persuasion (*describing* and using the *stated* outcomes from the environment and disregarding any social outcomes) became prevalent in Western history, and ushered in a new era during which the use of non-logical or non-rational ways to draw conclusions or to persuade people were considered highly negative, *and often punished*, even though all you are doing is taking into account the social outcomes of what is happening. And ever since, acting in 'non-rational' and 'non-logical' ways have variously been punished, negatively labelled, laughed at, or used as a reason to exclude or control people. When someone says, "You're not being rational!" it is a slur and the *likely positive social outcomes* for what was being suggested (why you were 'irrational') are not taken into account.

The big problem with this, though, is that the use of social relationships in influence has always had a different purpose than describing correct consequences from the non-social environment, and these are usually just as important for our lives as 'rational' reasons. By excluding social forms of influence, many other extremely important social and community functions have therefore also been excluded, and, as I just mentioned, these functions are often more important than being correct all the time. This has been the cost or collateral damage of promoting rationality in so many domains of life—*being exclusively rational weakens social relationships and these are often more important that the non-social outcomes.*

To look at this another way, the social forms of persuasion in general have to do with maintaining and solving conflicts in *social and community relationships*, and surely, doing that is actually being quite rational! The point that will be made in what follows, across several life domains that have been artificially restricted to rationality and logic, is that *excluding the social is itself actually not rational* at all, since it excludes social consequences that are vital in our real-world lives, but it has worked because of the fragmentation of social relationships already within capitalism, bureaucracy, and modernity. You should believe the saying, "Sticks and stones may break my bones but names will never harm me", at your own risk; look at the damage of the *Diagnostic and Statistical Manual of Mental Disorders* (DSM) labels (see Guerin, 2017, V6).

If, instead, we consider that social and community relationships are really part of our environment too, then it is still rational in a strict sense to pay attention to their consequences. The usual sense of 'rational' that was promoted only works by treating social and community relationship outcomes as not part of the environment (and treating money falsely as if it were non-social). That is fine if you are dealing with science, when your main concern is the non-social real world, but not in the other domains of life. And the big problems really happen when you then try to study social and community relationships 'scientifically'—that turns into a real mess if we only consider the non-social outcomes of social and community relationships to be important. This has led to all sorts of scientific dead-ends trying to reduce everything that arises socially from a non-social outcome in the environment (Bentall, 2006; Correia, 2013; de Montesquieu, 1987; Harris, 1979; Khaldun, 1967; Newman, 2013). This has been a major problem of modern psychology, which always falls back to future promises of brain processes.

In essence, this is the whole crux of this book: *trying to take the 'social' seriously again as a real environmental/contextual outcome in itself* (even though it is more difficult to observe), and then reanalysing some strategies that claim to be purely individual matters. Debates usually separate the 'environmental' world from the 'human' world, or some metaphorical equivalent of this, but the distinction itself needs to be changed. This is the basis also of both the false mind–body and nature–nurture splits (Descola, 2013).

We have 'advanced' or become 'civilized' as a species on this planet, but only by disregarding the important outcomes of social and community relationships and concentrating on gaining from the environmental resources. This has only seemed acceptable because our social relationships have been replaced by monetary relationships or contractual relationships, but monetary relationships are still social. If money were to lose its 'exchange value', most stranger relationships would stop. But we need to connect our everyday social relationships back to the societal structures that constrain those relationships, if we are to transform people and save the planet.

Table 1.1 shows the basic idea I have been describing over several domains of life, which will each then be briefly discussed. Note that they are all, except for some uses of science, really concerned with using rationality to gain resources and capital and to govern people through social organization. Some scientists are genuinely trying to be truthful by sticking to what they record about environmental observations and not be persuaded by the social outcomes of their talk, but this is more complex when trying to work in the domain of people—social and community relationships—since social outcomes need to be taken seriously in themselves, especially when it seems that a glaringly obvious environmental outcome must be the most important thing. As just mentioned, capitalist and neoliberal economics only gets away with this by (falsely) treating money and capital as non-social entities (Guerin, 2016a).

Science

Science has always been thought of as perhaps the one domain in which we need to pay attention to the 'rational' environmental outcomes very strictly; to believe what the data tell us, not what someone just says is true or wants us to say. And I agree with this in principle. But we are now seeing bad outcomes of this in environmental degradation from not paying attention to at least *some* of the social outcomes when messing with the environment (mostly through the perils and pitfalls from V4.7). And there are a few areas in which this causes problems, even for science.

The problem revolves around this claim: "Believe what the data tell us, not what someone just says is true or wants us to say". Just as I do not learn the word 'cat' from looking at cats, but from talking to people (V4.3), so what science *does*, does not *give* us any words. The phrase "what the data tell us" is fictional. We, as social humans do the telling, not the data.

Data are just events that we can observe; the 'telling' is about people; the 'telling' is never true or false but just does things to other people. This

Table 1.1 Nine domains of knowledge that have excluded the 'social', with examples of discourses of the 'rational' and the 'irrational', and how the 'social' should be highlighted

Domain of knowledge	Discourses of the rational	Discourses of the irrational, non-rational, or actual social and community contexts	Proper contextual role of the social
Science	Following rationality and logic, except in theorizing and modelling (which are also the most open to social disputes and conflicts between scientists) When intervention results are not certain, then social dogmatism can occur	Supernatural, unscientific, pseudo-science Witchcraft, sorcery	Sophisticated social strategies for solving resource and relationship problems within communities and families The language of science is still based on social outcomes and so is contestable and messy, but the observations, if done properly and over time, are not
Mental health	Behaving 'functionally' (DSM) In line with Western middle-class standards Behaving rationally and neoliberal	Insanity Non-functional Dysfunctional Mental illness Mad Crazy	The behaviours leading to the suffering primarily arise from hidden social and community events
Economics	Maximizing profit Money and its behaviour represented as non-social objects or events Rational economic theory Rational decision-making Social only included if put in terms of monetary 'value'	Irrational economics Biases in decision-making Dysfunctional cognitive processes Uneducated	Resource distribution by sharing Using community and social relationships in resource distribution Community decision-making and planning over resource distribution Non-profit means of resource distribution The social force needed to impose rational economics Money as a thoroughly social product

The opposite of rational is social   13

Law	Following the Westminster legal system of contract and tort Rational guidelines of argument in court Shaped purely for a society of strangers Not allowed to be influenced by social concerns Context no excuse for individual behaviour, thereby excluding social context	Biased, 'primitive law' Ritual, witchcraft, sorcery Understanding how people's behaviour arises in context excuses some responsibility	Sophisticated social strategies for solving resource and relationship problems within communities and families Non-rule ways of solving conflictual situations Communities and societies take some responsibility for any bad behaviours of individuals
Government and bureaucracy	Bureaucratic rule following, efficiency, austerity, neoliberalism, everything run in terms of written verbal rules	'Bludgers' Welfare dependency Rebels Nomads Anarchists Cheating the system	Community ways of caring for people and helping people in need of resource distribution Alternative social responsibility
Ecology	Animals, plants, and the planet are resources to be used One basis for capital generation and creating wealth Treat nature as a stranger/contractual relationship	Wasted resources Locked-up profits Backwards Non-civilized Non-progressive	Social, community, and spiritual uses (not all involving consumption) Sustainability Treat nature as a real relationship of family or friendship
Religion	Theology Atheism Doctrine Can be dogmatic when the non-social world contradicts Focus on what religion can gain for individuals	Supernatural Ritual Superstitions Pseudo-science Witchcraft, sorcery, primitive Faith-based beliefs and ideas	Community ways of caring for people and helping people in need of resource distribution Focus on what religion can gain for communities and social relationships, not the scientific accuracy of what is said

(continued)

Table 1.1 Cont.

Domain of knowledge	Discourses of the rational	Discourses of the irrational, non-rational, or actual social and community contexts	Proper contextual role of the social
Logic and Western philosophy	Logic is said to be context-free and so can give pure truths Following logical arguments only, without social bias Analysing the uses of language and where this is biased	Illogical, stupid, irrational, deficient Biases of rational arguments (ad hominem, circular argument, strawman argument, appeal to ignorance, hasty generalization, red herring fallacy, etc.)	Any social outcomes for the premises are excluded so logic only pretends to be context-free Ignores how the argument premises are 'established' or 'agreed' since these are social persuasion Often left as "I cannot see how …" Assumes wrongly that language can be true or false, rather than being a social behaviour that has effects on people
Psychology in the 1960s	The word 'information' was used to refer to events for people but with the social shapers removed Information is 'extracted' from the environment and becomes social-free and 'processed' in the brain Most psychologists assume that what we think controls our behaviour	'Emotions' interfered with correct 'information processing' so cognitive processing was called 'dysfunctional' when not matching rational models	All humans do is actually social (V4) Chapter 6 has more about our behaviour *not* being controlled by our rational thinking

is true for physics and chemistry as it is for psychology and the social sciences, and we must contextualize the research methods to account for this (see Chapter 9, Table 9.1).

These problems apply even to the 'hard' sciences. Scientists poke and prod the world and observe (with some errors unless you are careful), and that is one activity. The *talking* about what was done and what was seen (disguised as 'what the data tell us') is another totally *social* event and open to all sorts of problems (V4.7). Western philosophy has been about "How can I make these science *sentences* as certain as what I observe?" but this is futile. Scientific sentences can be neither falsified nor truthified! All they can do is to get other scientists to do things; that is all words can ever do.

The first problem area for science occurs when we do *not* have the data or good observations but scientists (or those who pay them) want to pretend to have a rational answer (which therefore cannot be socially disputed). That is, *the social seeps into science* especially when constructing theories, models, and metaphors, because we usually construct these exactly when we do *not* have good environmental observations, for whatever reason (e.g. Latour & Woolgar, 1986). This is exactly what Pathway 1 has done with modern psychology (V4.1), trying to appear as if it cannot be socially challenged because it is claimed to be a 'science': "We know this works for people because we have scientific proof" (see Chapter 9, Table 9.1).

This is where the brute rationality of science cannot be used because we do not actually know what the environment does at this point, and so all theories or models are solely and completely *social talk* (Kuhn, 1962). That is, when our observations are most decontextualized, that is precisely where we are most likely to find both theories and models used and also where we will find *social talk disguised as rational, scientific talk* (and therefore disagreements among scientists, V6.1). The use of theories and models is not a problem in itself, since they can be helpful to locate new observations and try doing new things to the world, but it is a problem when scientists are pressured to act as if their theories and words are being determined purely by environmental outcomes ('what the data tell us'), or when they become dogmatic about their theories. Theories are there to get other scientists *to do something new* with respect to the environment, not to 'represent' the world as truth.

A second problem for science, touched on briefly earlier, is from the long history of acting in the same 'rational' way when attempting to study people, communities, and society in a 'scientific' way; that is, trying to understand the social purely by how the environment affects people and paying less attention to the social and cultural contexts in which people are immersed, or assuming that they have little real consequences (see Chapter 9, Table 9.1). As already mentioned, these forms of reductionisms range from deriving all of society from differences in geography and temperature of regions (de Montesquieu, 1987; Khaldun, 1967), to deriving all human behaviour from physical substrates in the brain (metaphorical and theoretical, not with observations; Guerin, 2016b). In essence, the mistake is to have environmental models of people's behaviour where the social contexts are not present. Gross forms of 'individualism' have been the primary way of doing this in Western capitalist societies. Explaining everything as originating in the (non-social) brain is the latest form of this.

The third problem, related to the above, comes from treating some common human explanations in the same way as 'scientific' explanations because of the powerful influence of rationality. So, for example, if an Indigenous community talks about lightening occurring because the gods are not happy, many (insecure) scientists jump on this and disparage such talk as pseudoscience, rubbish, or primitive superstition. They do this because there are no environmental outcomes specified that determine the lightening, as happens for explanations from physics, for example.

Now, I am not trying to rubbish the scientific explanations, but there are two common issues that arise. First, for some of these common explanations, 'science' does not have a very good explanation grounded in observations either, and such scientists are inappropriately protecting their *talk* rather than their *actions or doing*. Indeed, there are some cases where the 'primitive superstition' proved true, particularly for herbal medicines. This, however, is not a rebuke of rational science itself but of those scientists who are arguing more confidently than is warranted by their own observations (this is really another example of the first problem just mentioned, scientists treating their *words* as non-social truths).

The second issue that arises is that for most of the 'primitive' and religious assertions, even when about the environment itself, having the correct environmental outcomes is not the focus of what is being said in any case. Instead, there are strong social and cultural outcomes for believing these 'wrong' assertions, which are vitally important for the community well-being regardless of any scientific truth (more in Chapters 5 and 8). Believing and ritually agreeing that lightening is about angry gods is part of the way such communities manage to work together and stay together, and these two outcomes are far more important than any rational truth about the explanation. *Getting explanations scientifically correct is not always the most important thing in life*, especially at the expense of communities, the survival of our environment, the continued existence of other species, or social relationships.

So, for me, what is happening here is that the scientists are actually showing their ignorance of the many social and community outcomes of spoken words and rituals, despite social anthropologists making these observations for decades. They are treating scientific statements as if they have some sort of direct connection to the non-social world, when in fact all words are social and never impinge directly on the non-social contexts of life.

As we will see in what follows, this also occurs for psychiatrists with 'mental health'; they are often not looking hard enough for *all the outcomes* of belief behaviours and are assuming that only a very limited range of outcomes (rational, environmental) are the only important ones (primarily the brain, see V6). They are dealing with what is *said* and very few contextual *observations*, even though talking has very different social outcomes (Guerin, 2016b).

So, we need to remember that when disparaging 'primitive' explanations as unscientific and not rational, the person saying this is really showing their ignorance of the social and community contexts and the vitally important *life outcomes* for agreeing with such explanations. This is not arguing that such explanations are therefore actually true with respect to the environment, but that they *are* probably functioning positively with respect to the social and community organization, and the over-enthusiastic scientists are missing totally this part of the equation of why such things are being said at all (Evans-Pritchard, 1937). The problem is that their own 'scientific statements' are also social and have no direct link to the world.

In summary, there is a cycle here that science works to observe and test the physical environment (this is good) but science also tries to put this into words (for other scientists to act, not for a statement of truth). This is best done if there are no social pressures applied to a scientific community such as Galileo experienced, especially when making observations. This works best for science if society as a whole believes the work of scientists rather than only what turns out to be useful. This in turn is best accomplished by having everyone usually follow any rule produced by science and believe it to be the best and most recent finding of 'knowledge'. So, while science can make mistakes in observations, someone who goes against scientific findings is not just going against that isolated finding, but against the whole community enterprise for setting up a useful, unbiased, and productive scientific community. This is why science often becomes a political issue (e.g. Gellner, 1992): because it is the community as a whole that maintains the scientific community from bias. So, such people get labelled as 'irrational' even in those case when science happens to be wrong.

The point of making non-social consequences the source of rationality, rather than whether or not something is 'rational', also helps solve the criticisms against rationality while retaining a sense of reality. Gellner (1992, p. 132), for example, provides a useful 'checklist of reason-bashing'. If reason and rationality consist of finding verbal reasons for doing something before acting, for example (Gellner, 1992, p. 132, item 2), then there is no certain rationality because the verbal behaviours themselves are determined by many social consequences. *Accepting that there are no certain or universal statements about rationality does not entail that there is no certain or universal observed reality, only that there are no certain language descriptions of reality.* 'Truth' is in the doing, not in the telling.

That is, we and all the other animals find our way around this world or perish, but we cannot put all of those contingencies that we contact into a verbal form that can always be perfectly followed, or that would always work out perfectly if they were followed (V4.7). The world is there and real, perfectly naked in its contingencies, but our verbal specifications of those contingencies are imperfect and following them depends upon many things, not least the community support for an unbiased science. We need to stop thinking of 'science' as the body of words (which are social behaviours to do things to other scientists) but as the observations of the world when we push and pull and prod it in new ways.

Mental health

Elsewhere (Guerin, 2017, V6) I have argued that by excluding or not spending the time to properly observe most of the societal and social contexts of a person's life, behaviours that seem unusual or that seem to occur without a context get labelled as 'mental health' issues, or insanity in the extreme. Further, the contexts excluded or not easily observed are mostly social, cultural, and language contexts, and so behaviours arising from these often do not make sense without the full context (since they are attuned to the affordances of people and not to the non-social world of physics). These, then, are typically the ones attributed to something about the person themselves—such as something wrong 'internally' or in a metaphorical domain called a 'mind', something about their race or culture, or about their brain or genes.

In earlier times, strange behaviours for which the context could not be easily observed might also have been said to be a result of something religious or supernatural. From the late eighteenth century, however, this became the bifurcate division between rational and irrational, or rational and insane. That is, if you were acting irrationally (i.e. not acting with respect to only the *obvious environmental consequences* of your actions or speech) then this would be attributed to some property about you labelled 'insanity'. However, the 'irrational' behaviour was really arising from the person's bad social and cultural situations (V6.3) and might have been quite rational when observed in social context properly, but this did not figure in the diagnosis and little effort was made to pursue such observations. Labelling was also easier so that people stopped looking for the (rational) hidden social or cultural contexts for these 'irrational' behaviours, especially once this process became ensconced within an asylum, a hospital, or a professional's clinical room.

One reason for all this, of course, was that the huge rise in stranger or contractual relationships in modernity, coupled with the demise of extended or kin-based relationships, meant that social context probably *was* more difficult to observe in this period of history. People typically knew how stress or conflict arose from within large families but not from the many stranger relationships in which they now had to engage. We can see with this the rise of stress, anxiety, and depression that appeared to have no basis in a person's context because they were arising from the pressure of amorphous and anonymous strangers in their worlds (Guerin, 2017, V6.1).

While the idea of 'insanity' or 'madness' has waned (Foucault, 2009), we now find the *equivalent* still fixed firmly in the modern world of capitalism and bureaucracy. Those acting with 'irrational' behaviours now get labelled as having 'mental health' issues when they are 'non-functioning', meaning that they can no longer participate in 'normal', rational (neoliberal, essentially) ways of modern life. This is exactly part of the criteria for almost every diagnosis in the DSM (American Psychiatric Association, 2013). We can be anxious and suffering because our mortgage payments have gone up, and that is artificially not labelled as mental illness; but if we can no longer 'function normally' with a job or pursuing education then this is attributed to a mental health problem. I argue that this is only because psychiatrists and clinical psychologists *do not look hard enough and long enough* for the social and cultural contexts from which these behaviours actually arise—and part of that, ironically, is the social context of trying to live in modernity.

So, this is one life domain where the rise of 'rational' behaviour was at the expense of observing social behaviour properly, and this has led in itself to much prolonged suffering. If someone cannot function in the modern world and is not acting 'rationally' with respect to the consequences *just* from the environment (they claim to see things that are not there), then they are irrational, mad, dysfunctional, or have mental health issues. The problem for us is that their behaviour actually *is* rational, but rational with respect to complex social and cultural outcomes that make up their bad situations in life (V6.3), but that are difficult to observe. Rather than tease out those social and cultural consequences for the odd behaviours we observe, we give a label or diagnosis instead. Some, of course, like Laing and Esterson (1964), did explore the contexts better to find out how the 'strange' behaviours arose within very subtle and complex family dynamics. But unlike this book, they did not pursue the effects of modernity, capitalism, and neoliberalism on their clients' behaviour (Smail, 2005; V6.7).

None of this means that the person with odd or 'irrational' behaviour is not suffering or in pain. It makes no difference that the behaviours are really arising from bad and complex social and cultural outcomes; the person is still suffering. My point is that rather than label the people involved as irrational or having mental health diseases, we need to explore, and make changes to, those social and cultural contexts if we wish to solve the life problems that are leading to their suffering (V6 does this in more detail).

The final point that comes up in each domain, is that the 'primitive' or religious explanations for the 'mental health' issues were treated as unscientific and ignored mostly. But we will see in what follows that they were there for other reasons (outcomes) as well, primarily social and community outcomes and therefore quite rational in the alternative way I have been describing (because including the real effects from social and community contexts is actually being rational). And the 'primitive' or religious interventions were likewise treated as 'superstitious' and irrational, but they actually had tremendously important social and community outcomes involved (these will be discussed more in V6.8).

Economics

From Adam Smith onwards, economics has also been dominated by similar forms of (non-social) rationality and rational thinking about dealing with money and commerce, and any influence from social outcomes over economic 'decisions' has been excluded or made secondary. As mentioned earlier, the numerical value of money has made it easy to exclude any social considerations from the basics of economics, because it appeared (falsely) that money was an external (non-social) part of our world and needed to be described as such.

What we call economics, however, is really only an extension of how people obtain and distribute the resources needed for life, and this has always been based on strong social considerations (Marx, 1809/1952; Simmel, 1907/1978). Under capitalism, as we have seen, the frequency and range of stranger relationships has grown enormously, and so economics (the social distribution of resources) has become a 'stranger trade' and treated outside of any social influences, leading to the very social exclusionary rational activity described in classical economic theory. This has also led to its basic competitive underpinning since, technically speaking, competition or zero-sum games are non-social. But this has been disastrous for real human beings living under strong capitalist systems and likely leads to all sorts of 'mental health' issues (Guerin, 2017).

For example, Box 1.2 shows some pre-capitalist communities in which food can be seen as a special resource that has almost *never* been treated by

Box 1.2 Food was not originally seen as tradeable or saleable

There is logic in an undue tendency to move food by generalized reciprocity. Like exchange between rich and poor, or between high and low, where food is concerned a greater inclination to sacrifice seems required just to sustain the given degree of sociability. Sharing needs to be extended to more distant relatives, generalized reciprocity broadened beyond ordinary sectoral limits ...

About the only sociable thing to do with food is to give it away, and the commensurably sociable return, after an interval of suitable decency, is the return of hospitality or assistance. The implication is not only a rather loose or imperfect balance in food dealing, but specifically a restraint on exchanges of food for other goods. One notes with interest normative injunctions against the sale of food among peoples possessed of primitive currencies, among certain Melanesian and California tribes for instance. Here balanced exchange is run of the mill.

Money tokens serve as more or less general equivalents and are exchanged against a variety of stuff. But not *food*stuff. Within a broad social sector where money talks for other things, staples are insulated against pecuniary transactions and food shared perhaps but rarely sold. Food has too much social value—ultimately because it has too much use value to have exchange value.

(Sahlins, 1972, pp. 217–218)

Food was not sold. It might be given away, but being "wild stuff" should not be sold, according to Pomo etiquette. Manufactured articles only were bought and sold, such as baskets, bows and arrows.

(Gifford, 1926, p. 329; cf. Kroeber, 1925, p. 40 on the Yurok)

[To the Tolowa-Tututni] food was only edible, not saleable.

(Drucker, 1937, p. 241; cf. DuBois, 1936, pp. 50–51)

The staple articles of food, taro, bananas, coconuts, are never sold [by Lesu], and are given to kindred, friends, and strangers passing through the village as an act of courtesy.

(Powdermaker, 1933, p. 195)

> In a similar way, staple foodstuffs were excluded from balanced trading among Alaskan Eskimo: "The feeling was present that to trade for food was reprehensible—and even luxury foods that were exchanged between trade partners were transferred as presents and apart from the main trading" (Spencer, 1959, pp. 204–205).
>
> It would seem that common foodstuffs are likely to have an insulated 'circuit of exchange', separate from durables, particularly wealth (see Bohannan, 1955; Bohannan & Dalton, 1962; and Firth, 1950 on 'spheres of exchange'). Morally and socially this should be so. For a wide range of social relations, balanced and direct food-for-goods transactions (conversions) would rend the solidarity bonds. Distinctive categorizations of food versus other goods, i.e. 'wealth' express the sociological disparity and protect food from dysfunctional comparisons of its worth—as among the Salish:
>
>> Food was not classed as "wealth" [i.e. blankets, shell ornaments, canoes, etc.]. Nor was it treated as wealth ... "holy food", a Semiahmoo informant called it. It should be given freely, he felt, and could not be refused. Food was evidently not freely exchanged with wealth. A person in need of food might ask to buy some from another household in his community, offering wealth for it, but food was not generally offered for sale.
>>   (Suttles, 1960, p. 301; see also Vayda, 1961)

them as a tradeable or saleable item at all, except occasionally to those who might be strangers (and even then, really for social reasons). Food was less about nutrition and what it did to the non-social environment of the body and was more about managing social and community commitments.

Providing food is now done completely for the monetary outcomes, and any important social outcomes, as just described, are ignored, disparaged, or played down. There is certainly nothing on the share markets about trading in food that is special or different to trading in washing machines. (However, a closely related phenomenon recently occurred in France. The French government made it illegal for supermarkets to throw away unsold food, which must now be given to the needy instead, a practice reminiscent of that detailed in Box 1.2 except that it had to be government mandated.)

More will be said later about the effects of modern economics, but the point here is that for a few centuries now, dealing with money and planning economies has worked within a rational model only, even though social consequences seep into this all the time (Marx, 1809/1952). But resource distribution is actually about people, social opportunities, and social inequalities in *all* its stages so we cannot really ignore describing the social consequences of economics, even though this is how it is currently done (Greer, 2011; Sandal, 2012; Stiglitz, 2013). And remember that modern economics is also built on an illusion that money acts as a non-social or environmental consequence of our actions, whereas money is really socially constructed and built through implicit agreements or contracts between strangers (Simmel, 1907/1978). We treat money like it 'grows on trees' in the sense that, unlike apples, we constructed money in the first place as a social behaviour and it is not provided on trees.

Law and legal systems

A similar story occurs for the development of Western forms of law, with one slight twist that will also reappear later for bureaucracies. In this case, the system over time became divorced from social influence, meaning that you could no longer use your family influence to sway the judge, or bully your way out of prison. But unlike science, the rationality in this case was underpinned by an adherence to verbal 'rules' rather than observations of the environmental consequences as science is supposed to do. That is, *rational law* was about following a series of written rules that specified what the outcomes would be in the (legal) world. Judges and juries *need to be rational by following the set rules and procedures*, those forming the laws of the particular land, rather than *giving in to social pressures*. They are not supposed to deviate from these in how they accuse and lay blame. Just as we have seen for money, these legal rules are treated as if they represent or come from the non-social environment rather than being socially constructed. But in most cases, they are not related to the reality since we do not spend much time observing what takes place following trials.

Once again, however, there is *seepage of the social into the rational*. In this case, seepage shows in the long-standing debates over subtle and gradual influences of 'public opinion' on laws (Dicey, 1905; Renner, 1949). That is, over time, the statutes about laws and sentencing can shift with public opinion (rather than with research observations). Likewise, prosecutors and defenders can use social methods of influence on judges and juries, but they have clearly defined limits and are supposed to stick with establishing 'rational' (that is, non-social) facts.

We again see that social influence is supposed to be excised from the proceedings, but gaps appear (V4.7). But we must remember that this was done for Western law that developed within a society of strangers, and that different outcomes, which are of extreme importance for smaller communities and kin-based societies, are no longer considered in a contractual society.

> The movement of the progressive societies has been uniform in one respect. Through all its course it has been distinguished by the gradual dissolution of family dependency and the growth of individual obligation in its place. The Individual is steadily substituted for the Family, as the unit of which civil laws take account ... Nor is it difficult to see what is the tie between man and man which replaces by degrees those forms of reciprocity in rights and duties which have their origins in the Family. It is Contract.
>
> (Maine, 1917, p. 99)

And just like all the cases earlier, there is a similar long history of treating 'primitive' law as superstitious, biased, and corrupt because social influences were taken seriously when determining guilt or innocence. Finding out whether someone was guilty of witchcraft, for example, by seeing whether a poisoned chicken lives or dies, is surely not rational (Evans-Pritchard, 1937; Tambiah, 1990). This prejudice continues today by treating many non-Western forms of laws in the same way, especially Indigenous laws that are perfectly 'rational' when the very real social consequences of judicial decisions are taken seriously once more.

But also, once again, we must reconsider the social contexts for 'primitive' law (Gluckman, 1972) and take seriously that the opposite of rational is social. Such 'primitive' law systems were made within kin-based communities and so, in addition to the outcome of finding the (non-social environment) truth about what happened, important outcomes for the whole community or families *needed* to be considered as part of the law. Western 'rational' law works by excluding any social outcomes as not important; but notice once again that this is really only viable within a society made up predominantly of stranger or contractual relationships where there are few real interdependencies between people. But for kin-based communities, there was no point in finding someone guilty if that then led to the break-up of the whole community. That would *not* be a rational thing to do, but this scenario does not occur in the same way with stranger relationships, so the Western law models can work up to a point.

> Furthermore, the analysis of judicial reasoning involves considering the types of social relations out of which the dispute has emerged. Among the Lovedu and Tiv, where most transactions take place between closely related persons, usually kinsmen or in-laws, if these sue each other the problems raised for judges must be different from those set judges who

are trying cases involving persons linked only by contract or tort, the common situation in Europe and America. Where closely related persons are involved, as among the Tiv, the judges may well try to *adjust their dispute so that they should be able to resume their friendly relationship* and it is a substantial advantage if all concur in the adjudication. This has been demonstrated often enough. Hence what we are shown is not that it is impossible to discuss African procedures and values in English, but that *if we want to understand African courts, we have to take into account the social relations on which they operate*. In fact, Bohannan's cases show that Tiv judges are more anxious to get the litigants' concurrence in cases involving blood-kin, than in cases involving strangers, or even in-laws whose relationship is about to break.

(Gluckman, 1965, p. 186, my italics)

In such cases, there is a very complex and *subtle* law system that not only takes the truth of what happened (environment) into account, but also the social contexts and even the future social contexts of the people involved. For the chicken example just mentioned, for instance, Evans-Pritchard (1937) showed that there were many flexible ways to adjust the results if crucial social and community relationships looked threatened by an outcome—the diviner could make a case that the amount of poison given to the chicken was not enough or was too much (of course, earlier similar examples exist in Western religious traditions of 'ordeals'; see Brown, 1975). This looks wrong, biased, and corrupt from a Western point of view but only because we are looking solely for the 'environmental truth' of the judgement, not the whole complicated social context of having to live and cooperate together as a community afterwards.

In fact, in Western systems, the judge and jury have no obligations to the defendant by design! So, this is different for Western courts not because we are more rational and wiser, but because the contractual or stranger relationships in our society are very different and it is easier to exclude the social consequences. But it frequently happens that the result of a Western, non-social adjudication leads to worse situations for all those involved afterwards, from both sides of the dispute and society in general. There are many and similar reasons for people trying to get the Western law systems to consider more *social justice* and not a rigid adherence to rules that pretend to come from the non-social world but were in fact made up.

Government and bureaucracy

Governing and organizing groups of people has also become rationalized in modernity. The total running of Western societies has been changed to rational and efficient models of bureaucracy (Weber, 1947). The more recent extreme is the entire governing by neoliberalism, that is, rational models for both economics and bureaucracies in the rational purge (Harvey, 2007; Hummel, 2014).

Once again, this works at all only because of the stranger or contractual relationships that now predominate in our lives. And once again, other beneficial social functions that could provide alternative and even better ways of organizing people have been lost by doing this. In particular, neoliberalism and bureaucracy have led to a marked weakening of smaller groups and communities trying to organize their own lives, since control over most of our lives is handed over to (or taken by) governments and bureaucracies. And finally, once again, 'primitive' forms of social life and governance are now not taken seriously, especially in the forcing (threatening) of Indigenous peoples in all colonized worlds to accept the Western forms of governance and repudiate their own, finely tuned, socially-based methods of organizing and managing community relationships (Behrendt & Kelly, 2008; Mbagwu, 2016; Walker, 1996). Doing this, as we now know, also accelerated the dissolution of Indigenous communities and social relationships.

Many people now think that basing government and economics purely on rationality and logic is not working, and everyday experiences are alienating people from any societal cooperation (Braedley & Luxton, 2010; Graeber, 2015; Harvey, 2007; Hummel, 2014; Merton, 1957; Ritzer, 1996, 1999; Sennett, 2006). In later chapters, I will look at some solutions people have suggested to this current state of modernity.

Ecology

Treating our environment in rational ways that exclude social outcomes might not be as readily apparent as the domains just covered, unless it is the realm of science. But there are several ways in which we can see that this has happened. I want to briefly mention one here, but there are others (Collard & Dempsey, 2017; Graham, 2015; Löwy, 2015, 2016; Mollison, 2002; Wallis, 2001).

The following was developed in a discussion with some friends at the University of Brasilia and a group of their students (I thank them for facilitating this). We were discussing the different social properties of different relationships (Guerin, 2016a; see also Chapter 3)—stranger/contractual, friends, family, kin-based—and the discussion then turned to environmental issues and how people might treat the environment around them in the same ways they are used to doing with their relationships.

I listed the rough ideas in Table 1.2. If we look at things this way, you can begin (re)thinking that people treat nature and the environment in the same way they generally treat other people.

Table 1.2 Properties of different forms of social relationships and how these are mirrored in our relationship with the natural environment

Relationships	Properties with relationships	Properties with ecology matched with properties of different social relationships)
Subsistence/ kin-based relationships	Treat environment, flora, and fauna as family or community	Obligations to environment Politeness Ancestors in environment Environment a living thing Ritual relationships Not easy to exit or ignore View as one system Everything viewed as social, part of social system and world
Family/friend relationships	Treat environment, flora, and fauna as part of your social network, with not too close ties and not with ties that will last over a long time	Use when necessary No long-term obligations Can exit Viewed as separate parts of networks Good relationships for entertainment Someone else can clean up the mess
Stranger/contractual relationships	Treat environment, flora, and fauna as contractual relationships, rationally, logically in terms of maximizing	No obligations beyond the immediate use or contract Can exit Not viewed as social at all Rationality excludes the social relationships

In subsistence times, with cooperative groups of people living in *kin-based* or *extended family relationships*, with all the properties these entail (see Chapter 3), this was how they treated the environment that provided all their resources, just like family and ancestors. Most 'tribal' groups would thank the animals they killed for food and apologize that they needed the meat to feed their families. They would look carefully after their land or country, and they would carefully monitor and watch over it. Subsistence groups would show a sense of obligation to the environment, a politeness, have rituals when they needed to use the environment, and treat it like a living entity rather than inert matter. It was seen as a large cooperative system that included humans and, like kin-based communities, it was difficult for them to ignore or exit from their environment (Brightment, Grotto, & Ulturhasheva, 2012; Costa & Fausto, 2010; Viveiros de Castro, 2015; Willerslev, 2007).

As individuals in modernity, some people now treat the environment like they treat *friendships*—they engage with it when it is useful for a particular resource that is needed, but do not help much with anything more chronic or that requires their long-term attention. A lot of the time the relationship with friends is used for *entertainment and distraction purposes* and this is how many people now treat the natural environment (e.g. climbing Uluru!). People can exit from modern friendships fairly easily and replace them with other substitutes. The environment is also often treated as if it is compartmentalized, like relationships in modernity, and the bigger systems picture of the environment is missing.

Other people also treat the environment and nature in the same way as they treat *strangers in contractual relationships*. They use it to gain money or capital, or if there is none of that, then they ignore it altogether. And beyond the money and capital contracts, they do not believe that they have any further obligations to the environment.

Religion and spirituality

I have already discussed rationality and religion earlier, when talking about science. Science has often been at the forefront of framing religions and spirituality as superstitious and irrational, and I have mentioned how this misses their main functions completely because the social outcomes (and social justice) are excluded from science. Weirdly, Christianity also became 'rationalized' during the Enlightenment and tried to mix rational (non-social) thought with religious thought (e.g. Thomas Aquinas and others; Siedentop, 2014), and thus was born the *theologies* of Christianity, which gradually became distanced from the real congregation members. This was then used to justify excluding Indigenous religions or spiritualties since there was no 'rational' theology attached to them, and the stated beliefs clearly went against both scientific and Christian thinking. The uses of 'rational' theology to justify abuses against Indigenous peoples by missionaries and others is well known (e.g. Lewis, 1988). They were seemingly oblivious to the important social functions they were destroying, all in the name of more environmental resources.

These topics will be discussed in more detail later (Chapter 8), so here I will just give some examples of the hidden positive social and community functions of such practices, which are ignored by 'rational' debates about religions and spiritualties. Here is a typical example, with the hidden social contexts given abstract labels of 'expressive' and 'symbolic':

> In my 1965 Malinowski Lecture I developed the theme that the ideas and procedures which we generally call "ritual" differ from those which we call "practical" and scientific (or "proto-scientific") in that they contain, or may contain, an expressive, symbolic quality, which is not found in technical thought or activity as such.
>
> (Beattie, 1970, p. 240)

All that is being said here is that the difference is not so large. Both ritual and practical activities are shaped by their consequences but the first is from social consequences that facilitate keeping communities and families together, while the latter from non-social environmental consequences. The social consequences are difficult to observe so they are given different ambiguous and abstract names: expressive, symbolic, meanings, mental associations, symbolic classifications.

The same applies for another general term for the opposite of rational, i.e. faith. The contrast is sometimes made between following rationality and following faith in a set of beliefs (not always religious). Faith, however, once again draws us back to social relationships and the shaping of such unexamined, faith-based beliefs by our groups for many outcomes. We could express faith to avoid punishment by those in our relationships, we could gain from expressing faith rather than the rational outcomes, or we could bond through expressing similar beliefs even if unexamined. But while faith might not be important in science experiments, it is important in holding communities and families together strongly and so *doing this is its very rational outcome* (Deloria, 1999, 2006).

A final example will bring out the same point we have seen throughout this chapter—that underlying these changes between science and religious practices was the rising Western propinquity of stranger relationships over family and kin-based relationships.

> This last point may provide the answer to the question why beliefs in witchcraft and sorcery, in the form in which they exist in many contemporary non-literate societies, have disappeared from our own society. We may attribute their disappearance, neither to the growth of religion, nor entirely to the rise in rationalism, but rather to the development of a society in which a large proportion of our day-to-day relationships are impersonal and segmental ones in which tension may be isolated and compartmentalized, and expressed in forms very different from those of a society small enough in scale to be dominated by the idea of personal influence.
>
> (Marwick, 1963/1967, p. 126)

Logic

Similar considerations apply to the rise of logic (more in Chapter 6). It is not that logic precludes considerations of social outcomes, but it disguises them. As I mentioned for Plato at the start of this chapter, logic only works once you have agreed premises, and getting agreement on premises is where the disguise, gap, or seepage takes place for the 'social' to sneak back in. Here are two examples, both pointed out in the 1880s by Nietzsche:

> On the origin of logic. The fundamental inclination to posit as equal, to see things as equal, is modified, held in check, by consideration of usefulness and harmfulness, by considerations of success: it adapts itself to a milder degree in which it can be satisfied without at the same time denying and endangering life. This whole process corresponds exactly to that external, mechanical process (which is its symbol) by which protoplasm makes what it appropriates equal to itself and fits it into its own forms and files.
>
> (Nietzsche, 1967, p. 510)

> Logic is subject to the following condition: suppose that there are identical cases. In fact, for there to be logical thought and inferences, this condition must first be treated fictitiously as fulfilled. That is: the demand for logical truth can only take place after a fundamental falsification of all events has been assumed.
>
> (Nietzsche, 1967, p. 512)

This goes back to the perils and pitfalls of using language (V4.7). Logic pretends to be context-free but the premises and assumptions to get this are false. See Chapter 6 for more on logic and dialectics.

References

American Psychiatric Association. (2013). *The diagnostic and statistical manual of mental disorders* (5th ed.). Washington, DC: APA.

Beattie, J. H. M. (1970). On understanding ritual. In B. R. Wilson (Ed.), *Rationality* (pp. 240–268). Oxford: Basil Blackwell.

Behrendt, L., & Kelly, L. (2008). *Resolving Indigenous disputes: Land conflict and beyond*. Sydney: Federation Press.

Bentall, R. P. (2006). Madness explained: Why we must reject the Kraepelinian paradigm and replace it with a 'complaint-orientated' approach to understanding mental illness. *Medical Hypotheses, 66*, 220–233.

Bloch, M. (Ed.) (1975). *Political language and oratory in traditional societies.* London: Academic Press.

Bohannan, P. (1955). Some principles of exchange and investment among the Tiv. *American Anthropologist, 57,* 60–70.

Bohannan, P., & Dalton, G. (Eds.) (1962). *Markets in Africa.* Evanston, IL: Northwestern University Press.

Braedley, S., & Luxton, M. (2010). *Neoliberalism and everyday life.* Montreal, Canada: McGill-Queen's University Press.

Brightment, M., Grotto, V. E., & Ulturhasheva, O. (Eds.). (2012). *Animism in rainforest and tundra: Personhood, animals, plants and things in contemporary Amazonia and Siberia.* New York, NY: Berghahn.

Brown, P. (1975). Society and the supernatural: A medieval change. *Daedalus, 104,* 133–151.

Brown, P. (1992). *Power and persuasion in late antiquity: Towards a Christian empire.* Madison: University of Wisconsin Press.

Collard, R. -C., & Dempsey, J. (2017). Capitalist natures in five orientations. *Capitalism Nature Socialism, 28,* 78–97.

Correia, D. (2013). F**k Jared Diamond. *Capitalism Nature Socialism, 24,* 1–6.

Costa, L., & Fausto, C. (2010). The return of the animists: Recent studies of Amazonian ontologies. *Religion and Society: Advances in Research, 1,* 89–109.

de Montesquieu, C. (1987). *The spirit of the laws.* Cambridge, UK: Cambridge University Press.

Deloria, V. (1999). *Spirit and reason: The Vine Deloria Jr reader.* Golden, CO: Fulcrum.

Deloria, V. (2006). *The world we used to live in: Remembering the powers of the medicine men.* Golden, CO: Fulcrum.

Descola, P. (2013). *The ecology of others.* Chicago, IL: Prickly Paradigm Press.

Dicey, A. V. (1905). *Lectures on the relation between law and public opinion in England during the nineteenth century.* London: Macmillan.

Drucker, P. (1937). The Tolowa and their Southwest Oregon kin. *University of California Publications in American Archaeology and Ethnology, 36,* 1–300.

DuBois, C. (1936). The wealth concept as an integrative factor in Tolowa-Tututni Culture. In A. L. Kroeber, *Essays presented to A. L. Kroeber.* Berkeley: University of California Press.

Evans-Pritchard, E. E. (1937). *Witchcraft, oracles, and magic among the Azande.* Oxford: Clarendon Press.

Firth, R. (1950). *Elements of social organization.* London: Watts.

Foucault, M. (1970). *The order of things: An archaeology of the human sciences.* London: Pantheon.

Foucault, M. (2009). *History of madness.* London: Routledge.

Gellner, E. (1992). *Reason and culture: The historic role of rationality and rationalism.* Oxford: Basil Blackwell.

Gifford, E. W. (1926). Clear Lake Pomo Society. *University of California Publications in American Archaeology and Ethnology, 18,* 287–390.

Gluckman, M. (1965). *Politics, law and ritual in tribal society.* Oxford: Basil Blackwell.

Gluckman, M. (Ed.) (1972). *The allocation of responsibility.* Manchester: Manchester University Press.

Graeber, D. (2015). *The utopia of rules: On technology, stupidity, and the secret joys of bureaucracy.* London: Melville House.

Graham, N. J. (2015). Ecological forces of production. *Capitalism Nature Socialism, 26,* 76–91.

Greer, J. M. (2011). *The wealth of nature: Economics as if survival mattered.* Gabriola Island, BC: New Society Publishers.

Guerin, B. (1995). Social influence in one-to-one and group situations: Predicting influence tactics from basic group processes. *Journal of Social Psychology, 135,* 371–385.

Guerin, B. (2003). Language use as social strategy: A review and an analytic framework for the social sciences. *Review of General Psychology, 7,* 251–298.

Guerin, B. (2016a). *How to rethink human behavior: A practical guide to social contextual analysis.* London: Routledge.

Guerin, B. (2016b). *How to rethink psychology: New metaphors for understanding people and their behavior.* London: Routledge.

Guerin, B. (2017). *How to rethink mental illness: The human contexts behind the labels.* London: Routledge.

Harris, M. (1979). *Cultural materialism.* New York, NY: Random House.

Harvey, D. (2007). *A brief history of neoliberalism.* London: Oxford University Press.

Hummel, R. P. (2014). *The bureaucratic experience: The post-modern challenge.* London: Taylor & Francis

Khaldun, I. (1967). *The Muqaddimah: An introduction to history.* Princeton, NJ: Princeton University Press.

Kroeber, A. L. (1925). *Handbook of the Indians of California. Smithsonian Institution Bureau of American Ethnology Bulletin 78.* Washington, DC: US Government Printing Office.

Kuhn, T. S. (1962). *The structure of scientific revolutions.* Chicago, IL: University of Chicago Press.

Laing, R. D., & Esterson, A. (1964). *Sanity, madness and the family.* London: Penguin Books.

Latour, B., & Woolgar, S. (1986). *Laboratory life: The construction of scientific facts.* Princeton, NJ: Princeton University Press.

Lewis, N. (1988). *The missionaries: God against the Indians.* London: Vintage.

Löwy, M. (2015). *Ecosocialism: A radical alternative to capitalist catastrophe.* Chicago, IL: Haymarket Books.

Löwy, M. (2016). For an ecosocialist ethics. *Capitalism Nature Socialism, 27,* 21–26.

Maine, H. (1917). *Ancient law.* London: Dent.

Marwick, M. G. (1963/1967). The sociology of sorcery in a Central African tribe. In J. Middleton (Ed.), *Magic, witchcraft, and curing* (pp. 101–126). Austin, TX: University of Texas Press.

Marx, K. (1809/1952). *Capital. Volume 1*. Chicago, IL: Encyclopaedia Britannica.
Mbagwu, J. (2016). *Indigenous approaches in resolving conflicts in Africa: Women and post-conflicts reconstruction*. Ibadan, Nigeria: Ababa Press.
Merton, R. K. (1957). *Social theory and social structure*. New York, NY: Free Press.
Mollison, B. (2002). *Introduction to permaculture* (2nd ed.). Sisters Creek, Tasmania: Tagari.
Newman, S. A. (2013). The demise of the gene. *Capitalism Nature Socialism*, 24, 62–72.
Nietzsche, F. (1967). *The will to power*. London: Penguin.
Plato (1997). *The dialogues of Plato*. Trans. B. Jowett. Chicago, IL: Encyclopaedia Britannica.
Powdermaker, H. (1933). *Life in Lesu*. New York, NY: Norton.
Renner, K. (1949). *The institutions of private law and their social functions*. London: Routledge & Kegan Paul.
Ritzer, G. (1996). *The McDonaldization of society*. Thousand Oaks, CA: Pine Forge Press.
Ritzer, G. (1999). *Enchanting a disenchanted world: Revolutionizing the means of consumption*. Thousand Oaks, CA: Pine Forge Press.
Ryle, G. (1971). *Collected papers. Volume 1: Critical essays*. London: Hutchinson.
Sahlins, M. (1972). *Stone Age economics*. London: Tavistock.
Sandal, M. J. (2012). *What money can't buy: The moral limits of markets*. London: Penguin.
Sennett, R. (2006). *The culture of the new capitalism*. London: Yale University Press.
Siedentop, L. (2014). *Inventing the individual: The origins of Western liberalism*. London: Penguin Books.
Simmel, G. (1907/1978). *The philosophy of money*. London: Routledge & Kegan Paul.
Smail, D. (2005). *Power, interest and psychology: Elements of a social materialist understanding of distress*. London: PCCS Books.
Spencer, R. F. (1959). *The North Alaskan Eskimo: A study in ecology and society. Smithsonian Institution Bureau of American Ethnology Bulletin 171*. Washington, DC: US Government Printing Office.
Stiglitz, J. E. (2013). *The price of inequality*. London: Penguin.
Suttles, W. (1960). Affinal ties, subsistence and prestige among the Coast Salish. *American Anthropologist*, 62, 296–305.
Tambiah, S. J. (1990). *Magic, science, religion, and the scope of rationality*. Cambridge, UK: Cambridge University Press.
Vayda, A. P. (1961). A re-examination of Northwest Coast economic systems. *Transactions of the New York Academy of Sciences* (Series 2), 23, 618–624.
Viveiros de Castro, E. (2015). *The relative native: Essays on Indigenous conceptual worlds*. Chicago, IL: Hau Books.
Walker, R. (1996). *Ngā pepa a Ranginui/The Walker Papers: Thought-provoking Views on the Issues affecting Māori and Pākehā*. Ringwood, Victoria: Penguin Books.

Wallis, V. (2001). Towards ecological socialism. *Capitalism Nature Socialism*, *12*, 127–145.
Weber, M. (1947). *The theory of social and economic organization*. Oxford: Oxford University Press.
Willerslev, R. (2007). *Soul hunters: Hunting, animism and personhood among the Siberian Yukaghirs*. Berkeley: University of California Press.

2 How are our behaviours shaped by societal 'systems' and 'structures'?

The questions of system theories and behavioural practices are really about the relation between societal 'systems' or 'structures' and how they impact and shape 'individual' behaviour. Each of these terms is in scare quotes because there are several ways they can be thought about. In particular, these nouns are usually nominalized and abstract, and this limits how we can think, research, and intervene if we need to progress from abstract 'entities' to more concrete behaviours.

The aim of this chapter is therefore to suggest some more concrete and observable ways we can conceptualize the links between societal 'systems' or 'structures' and people's observable behaviours. In carrying out this aim there are three main questions:

- What is the status or reality of systems and structures?
- What is the status or reality of an individual and their behaviours?
- How do the systems or structures actually shape or impact on the individual's actions, talking, and thinking?

After introducing the area further, the chapter will discuss these in turn and conclude with some examples of concrete links from research between what a 'society' does (whether in terms of structures or systems), and what individuals do.

How do we get from sociological to 'individual'?

There is a long history in the social sciences of finding ways to describe the influence of widespread societal structures and ideologies on the behaviour of individuals. In psychology, this has mainly been done by passive and abstract theorizing, such as claiming that people have a 'tendency' to follow social norms or to copy their identity/reference groups, (Bentley, 1895; Guerin, 2016a). This sometimes gives the impression that people just automatically follow the societal norms, rules, or customs, and early psychologists even wanted to label these as instincts or drives (herd instinct, crowd instinct, cooperative instinct; McDougall, 1923). These are all tautologies.

Pathway 1 (V4.1) in psychology also allowed a cheating way: it did not matter what a society did, how the 'individual' thought about and 'processed' this was most important and predictive (also see Chapter 8), and clinical psychology has also followed this wrong 'fork in the road' (V6.1). To merge psychology into the social sciences, we need to change all these discursive cheats.

Some *observations* for talking in this way certainly seem correct, since there is much homogeneity when one observes people's behaviour with a broad sweep and without looking at the micro details too much. But all this talk is very misleading, however, because 'social norms' are defined in the first place as those behaviours people do frequently and in common, so we cannot then use 'social norm' as a *cause* or an *explanation* of those same behaviours. This applies to the other types of theoretical structures or systems: class, personality, etc. For example, we can observe similar behaviours among a community of people (such as an accent) and nominalize this as a class structure, but we cannot then explain those behaviours by appealing to that structure (Gerth & Mills, 1953).

The observations mentioned, however, are very broad. Those who look at more of the details of everyday life also see people behaving outside the 'norms', they see revolutions large and small that change the norms, and they see the daily struggles of people who are suffering from the social norms but try without success to change them (V6.3). As well, different societies and cultures (broadly used; V2.7) have very different social norms, which suggests that norms are more fluid than they sometimes appear. And the 'cultural' norms of smaller groups can also be observed to change if you look at more details over time rather than as a snapshot (Barth, 1987; Bloch, 1992; Festinger, Riecken, & Schachter, 1956; Firth, 1960; Harrison, 1992; Kolig, 1984).

The problem so far is about how we identify the societal structures and systems in the first place: the abstract nature of our talk about such structures, and the dangers of tautologous explanations arising from this. Societal structures and systems must have concrete and material effects that potentially can be observed affecting individuals (see Chapter 3), but this requires a change of vision, and research methodologies.

This chapter will explore further how we can pull apart and describe more closely the contexts for societal structures and systems that engage with individuals. Where should we look when observing people, since the societal structures are not obviously emblazoned or stamped on either our behaviour or on our environments? How can we 'see' the influence of the society, the economic systems, the patriarchy, and the bureaucratic systems when we simply watch individuals behaving in their concrete worlds? How can psychologists and clinical psychologists get a 'sociological imagination' (Mills, 1959)?

Is there even an individual?

One of the problems in considering the issues of this whole book is that people are invariably considered in Western thought as self-contained and self-animated 'individuals' (Guerin, 2001). Sociology and psychology have therefore usually pitted the individual *against* society whereas we need to consider them together—*people and 'society' are one material mass, they are a single set of events.* If they are separated in our words and theories, then the environment must somehow 'enter' into people at some distinct point. Most models at this point require that something 'in' the individual reacts to the environment rather than observing and describing exactly where the environment shapes those 'reactions' in the first place.

> The influence of environment upon the human mind has always been recognized by psychologists and philosophers; but it has been considered a secondary factor. On the contrary the social medium which the child enters at birth, in which he lives, moves and has his being, is fundamental. Toward this environment the individual from childhood to ripest old age is more or less receptive; rarely can the maturest minds so far succeed in emancipating themselves from this medium as to undertake independent reflection while complete emancipation is impossible, for all the organs and modes of thought, all the organs for constructing thoughts, have been moulded or at least thoroughly imbued by it. Granted that very mature and independent thinkers have passed the age of receptivity, still it is questionable whether the most eminent and original philosopher in the world can so far dissociate himself from the acquired modes and organs as to substitute independent creations in their place.
> (Gumplowicz, 1885/1980, pp. 240–241)

In terms of how individuals are already part of societal structures and systems, and the 'individual' is a fiction, it is interesting that a nineteenth-century *sociologist* (Gumplowicz, 1885/1980) should write in this vein, at the very same time when psychology was in the process of proposing the exact opposite as the 'scientific' path to follow (Wundt; Pathway 1, see V4.1). Even in behaviour analysis, one form of psychology that has doggedly pursued environmental determinants of behaviour, it was probably the form of the experimental chamber, with a clearly differentiated individual (rat) and environment (cage), which suggested the 'lines of natural fracture' that still pitted an organism against the environment (Skinner, 1935, p. 40). This made sense in the chamber and produced an important line of research, but this 'natural fracture' is not at all clear when we are researching humans and their place in societal structures and systems. We need to be prepared to analyse environments in another way, and to use different methods to observe and describe these environments.

The real problem is that few have actually carefully described in detail all the 'environments' for humans (attempts are compiled in Guerin, 1994, 2004, 2016c). Rather than adding more layers of *talking* about societal structures and systems, it is our methods for observing that we need to change (Table 9.1). We need to find observable effects of society and to denominalize 'societal structures and systems' through observation rather than more and more categories. In principle, behaviour analysis and social contextual analyses are well placed to achieve this since, like social anthropology and some sociology, small samples with intensive observations have been preferred (Guerin, 2018; Guerin, Leugi, & Thain, 2018).

What this means is that we should think of people as already 'in' or 'part of' the societal systems and structures. Everything they do, say, and think has already been shaped by these structures even when difficult to observe. This is the use of our 'sociological imagination', in which most psychologists are not trained (Mills, 1959). Even the most 'inner' reactions of people, their thinking, is already in the environments not inside them (V4.4).

> The great error of individualistic psychology is the supposition that man thinks. It leads to the continual search for the source of thought in the individual and for the reason why the individual thinks so and not otherwise; and prompts naive theologians and philosophers to consider and even to advise how man ought to think. A chain of errors; for it is not man himself who thinks but his social community; the source of his thoughts is in the social medium in which he lives, the social atmosphere which he breathes, and he cannot think ought else than what the influences of his social environment concentrating upon his brain necessitate. There is a law of mechanics and optics by which we compute the angle of refraction from the angle of incidence and in the realm of mind there is a similar law though we cannot observe it so exactly. Every ray of thought falling in on the mind is reflected in our views. What we think is the necessary result of the mental influences to which we have been subjected since childhood ... The individual simply plays

How are our behaviours shaped? 39

the part of the prism which receives the rays, dissolves them according to fixed laws and lets them pass out again in a predetermined direction and with a predetermined color.

(Gumplowicz, 1885/1980, p. 240)

This follows nicely from many behavioural and contextual analyses in which the basic unit is the whole contingency, interbehaviour, or 'field', rather than distinct stimuli, responses and consequences. These give the flavour that societal structures and systems are not 'taken into' the organism but are already part and parcel of the basic units (V4.5). The question, therefore, is how to describe these as a whole. Where do people fit into the societal systems and structures, and vice versa? How do we observe these? How do we change these?

Where do societal systems and structures come from?

The first problem to solve is what we need to observe if we wish to observe the 'societal structures and systems' as concrete instances, and to denominalize them. This section will discuss the nature of societal structures and systems in terms of their *functioning*, to assist in denominalizing them through observation (rather than through yet another conceptual scheme). If they remain as abstract 'entities' that do not change and that have not arisen from some functioning then it is unlikely we can get far. The following section will then give examples of how we can observe these. We can learn most by the contextual experts: social anthropologists for the kin-based communities and participatory sociologists for Western societies.

A starting point is the succession of disputes throughout the social sciences about *structure versus function*. This has plagued the history of social anthropology, sociology, and psychology (e.g. Rappaport, 1984). In psychology and linguistics, the famous case is of the structural grammar and linguistics of Chomsky 'versus' the functional linguistics of Firth, Skinner, Halliday, and others. In fact, there are many structures that have been proposed in the social sciences and all have similar problems (Rappaport, 1984, Appendix).

When measured over large numbers of people, most of the proposed 'societal structures' have some predictive research value for human behaviour, but they are also well known for tautologically becoming explanations, as discussed earlier in this chapter. For example, the commonly occurring grammatical 'structures' are real and observable, but small-scale exceptions or variations are ignored or denied (Everett, 2005), and grammatical structures are then tautologically used to *explain* how people use language.

The main cases of societal structures and systems relevant to human behaviour are:

- class structures;
- race structures;
- gender structures;
- economic structures;
- social structures;
- family structures;
- personality structures;
- social norms;
- hereditary structures;
- bureaucratic structures;
- cultural structures;
- linguistic structures;
- social roles.

These structures or systems all show similar problems when you look more closely at the context or detail. To break these down into observables it is important to first find the function that goes with their structure, rather than to oppose function and structure. To accomplish this, it is useful to think of 'structures' as slow-changing, repetitive, or static functions: "Structures are ossified functions" (Guerin, 1994, p. 107). This reanimates the nouns and provides us with potentially non-abstract events to observe, potential avenues for exceptions to the rules, and ways to try and change the structures where appropriate (V6.7).

If the outcomes of actions that shape similar future actions (their functions) are *repetitive*, *static*, or *slow changing* then they will be observed or measured *as if they were object-like*. This is the same for those that are *easily observable* and those that are not (mountains versus patriarchal structure). This has led to theorizing these structures as if they really were objects ('social facts'; e.g. Durkheim, 1982), which has been misleading or vague in so many ways for the social sciences because as soon as the functioning or outcomes of those events that shape them are changed, those 'structures' will change.

As mentioned earlier, the structural approaches can certainly predict behaviours in the short term, especially with combined data from many individuals, but even then, *such structural predictions only work if the environmental outcomes remain in place and are repetitive*. The functionality inherent in any structures that are found therefore needs more analysis on the part of researchers, to show how these structures come to be observed in the first place. Much of real life escapes these social and societal structures but is lost both in aggregate data and when structures are nominalized.

So, rather than leading to theories of 'objective social structures', what these observed structures should really throw up for research are these different questions:

- Why are the outcomes or functions static or slow changing in the first place?
- Where and when have these functions changed in the past or in other contexts?
- How can we or something else change these static forms of functioning and thus change the structures that have been observed?

Here lies the crux of the issue. Social science talks about social and societal structures of all the different forms listed earlier, therefore:

- *Predictions* can only be made of a gross nature, and not for individuals.
- The potential avenues for *changing* those structures or systems are not made clear and are hidden.
- We are not fully *understanding* what is going on because the structure is just assumed to be there like an object in the first place (even mountains wear away eventually).

On the other hand, when we have a highly functional approach such as in behavioural or contextual analysis, it is more difficult to *predict* over many different contexts, it appears that the outcomes can always be *changed* because changing the functioning environments have been simplified, and we are not fully *understanding* what is going on because the real-world structures are not so simple to modify.

I will give an example of each, showing the complexities. First, we can make good predictions of many social behaviours and linguistic accents over large social groups by using 'class structure' as a predictor (sociolinguistics and some social psychology). However, nothing in our research shows what the class structure is and how it was shaped functionally, which means that we do not learn anything about changing the class structures or even how people engage with them when their accents are being shaped. Second, in an operant laboratory we can shape clean, predictive behaviour patterns (variable interval (VI) schedules, fixed ratio (FR) schedules) by varying the outcomes/consequences, and can easily see how we change the behaviour by changing these outcomes. However, none of this helps us understand what the large, shaping structures of real life actually already are and whether there is any real chance of changing them, and this means that the patterns found in the laboratory cannot be considered 'foundational', 'basic', or 'building blocks' of any other behaviour patterns outside of that set-up.

So, the problem is that we have studied either fluid functions or static structures and both have been successful in some ways, but most of real life is in the middle. We know that food as a reinforcement for hungry organisms can function to rapidly change behaviour, and we know that the patriarchal structures and systems shape strong and differential behaviours in men and women that are difficult to change. What we do *not* know is (1) what apart from food is reinforcing all the rest of our behaviours (or even if the term 'reinforcing' is useful anymore), or (2) what has shaped that patriarchal structure or system into place since it is not permanent but just an ossified function that looks like a noun, and how these actually shape individuals.

As suggested earlier, the solution to this, I believe, is not to have more words about structures versus functions, *but to resolve by observation*:

- While accepting the results of experimental functional studies, question how a person's actual world is structured into the outcomes that shape them; the two might not match since the it is the researcher who structures the outcomes in a laboratory in the first place.
- While accepting the generic predictions of real societal structures and systems, question what material presence shapes the individual's behaviour rather than abstract terms.

These two, of course, go together, and it all depends upon the *stability* of those structures (like mountains versus lava), and that depends on what repetitive functioning produces those structures. If the functioning (the outcomes that occur) of the structures changes then the structures will change and no longer be predictive.

How do societal systems and structures impact on 'individual' behaviour?

The big questions, therefore, are how to identify the repetitive functioning that produces structures that 'look like' objects, and how these in turn change. A lot of useful answers come from sociology and social anthropology, which have already grappled with these questions, much more than psychology that answers by claiming unobservable structures internal to the individual, usually located in the brain (V4.1). In fact, since Wundt there has been an assumption in psychology that there is an internal and *unchanging* processing structure that deals with any material passing through the senses (Guerin, 2016b). Such material is 'cognitively processed' or formed into *associative structures* but the processing structures themselves are said to be unchanged, like an industrial assembly conveyer belt. Such solutions are unobservable and theoretical only (V4.8).

From sociology and social anthropology, we get more useful suggestions. In human terms, the functional outcomes are clearly dependent upon *resource distributions* through society or social groups, and so societal structures and systems must rest upon these. These can then be made even more concrete by examining the resource *opportunities* available to individuals in any societal environment and how the societal structures and systems are *stratified* across groups of people. You can go even further by looking at the *stability* over time of the opportunity contexts or environments, to explain why some structures seem static and therefore object-like and unchanging. In most cases these indeed match with the theoretical forms of societal structures and systems. Western society is said to be *stratified* across class, race, and gender, for example, and there are proposed *structures* of class, race, and gender in society.

With better observations of resource distribution, opportunities, and stratification we hope to more easily observe the ways in which functioning for individuals is patterned or shaped by 'structures' since individuals can only engage with what is available. Just pointing out this one link between societal structures or systems from resource distributions, opportunities, or stratifications, and individual behaviours, however, does not immediately help anything. While most behaviour is certainly shaped by its consequences, knowing this tells us nothing about what consequences actually exist for humans, how they are arranged (structured) across social groups, what research methods we might use to observe them, or how we might change these in any case. What we still need to do is to observe and describe these structural resource distributions, opportunities, or stratifications even if they are difficult to change.

Examples of deconstructing some 'psychological' structures and systems

Grammar

Grammar shows very consistent structures across large groups of people. Even when languages differ (English has a broad subject–verb–object (SVO) structure and German has subject–object–verb (SOV)) there is strong consistency within a language. This therefore *appears* as an 'object-like' structure that comes from nowhere (Chomsky even said it was hard-wired) and does not—or cannot—be changed. What we really need to look at closer is the question of *why the grammatical functionality is so static within our linguistic or discursive communities*. Notice, however, that this does not deny that there is grammatical structure.

A possible answer I have suggested (Guerin, 1997) lies in the *social importance* for our lives of maintaining strong, easily heard (discriminable), and easily responded to patterns of language. That is, having grammatical structures (that are repeatable and static) functions by allowing us to respond more easily to language—smoothly, quickly, and with few mistakes. Therefore, it is vitally important for all aspects of our lives (both getting resources and making social relationships) that linguistic communities do not alter this grammar in any way or else language use would slow down and many more mistakes would occur. You can try this yourself by changing your grammar and watching your listeners.

That is, we need to have purely repetitive outcomes (functions) from grammar or else the language becomes slow and difficult, and in material terms, our resources and social relationships suffer. If English speakers began randomly to switch between SVO and SOV it would be a mess and likely create problems in our lives. This is why it *looks* hard-wired but the strong structure comes from the *social importance* of maintaining a strong pattern of functional outcomes. One link to individual behaviour, therefore, is that we get both most of what we need and our social relationships through language use (V4.3), so messing up the grammar would in turn mess these up.

So, researchers in sociolinguistics find 'stable' structures in language use (like Chomsky said), but these are stable only if they remain functional. Using a consistent grammar is functional because if you stop using the 'standard' grammatical structures you will lose the many social and resource outcomes that language provides, or they take longer to get. Chomsky and others just assumed that the structures would go on and on forever. But languages change when the communities of speakers change.

'Personality'

When a person starts repeating a habitual pattern of responding, psychologists commonly talk about a 'personality structure'. What this really means is that *the person's environments or lifeworlds are static or only slowly changing*, and so the output for what they do remains the same over time, so they repeat those 'habits' over and over. If the behaviours thus shaped are dysfunctional in other ways, then psychiatrists will even talk about 'personality disorders'. But the 'disorder' is in the way the bad societal functioning is occurring and in the way it has become static or only slowly changing.

So ironically, 'personality structures' are external to the person (cf. Gerth & Mills, 1953). If someone has a 'strong personality', whether good or bad, this means that they have a static lifeworld controlling their resourcing and social relationships. If someone has a 'borderline personality' this means that they have been immersed in a 'borderline set of functionalities' produced by their society (Fromene & Guerin, 2014). The stability of so-called 'personality' is in the stability of their worlds.

Social structures

Structures of social groups or societies, in this approach, closely depend upon the ecology or the regularity of producing the resources needed for life. In 'tribal' life, the ecologies were tracked over generations and so clear social structures were produced—food ecology just kept on repeating the same way year by year. *Stable ecologies allowed stable social structures* to remain in place, and so anthropologists could map the strongly patterned structures of community and family life easily. But *social structures change when the ecology changes* (Barth, 1987; Bloch, 1992; Evans-Pritchard, 1965; Festinger et al., 1956; Firth, 1960; Geertz, 1973, p. 170; Harrison, 1992; Kolig, 1984; Leach, 1954; Strecker, 1988; Wilson, 1969, p. 371). Detailed anthropological evidence shows that even community rituals track the current social vicissitudes and are actively used for changing and organizing social groups (Barth, 1987; Bloch, 1992; Geertz, 1973; Leach, 1954; Strecker, 1988; Wilson, 1969).

In the modern world, it is the 'ecology' of capitalism that now determines our outcomes or life resources, and this has also set up some regularities, including differences between work done (the class 'structures' arising from the divisions of labour'), gender structures, race structures, etc. Likewise, 'social norms' have been observed as static for periods but regularly changing as Western societies have changed (more in Chapter 3).

Patriarchy

Similarly, for patriarchal 'structures', males and females learn to get different but predictable outcomes for the very same behaviours, and this shapes their future behaviours, but this is not about inherent male and female differences. Our society has fixed repetitive ways of making opportunities or privileges easy for some and not others, and so this looks like a permanent, 'objective' structure'. But it is just the way the environment is currently programmed for the outputs of behaviours and we can in principle change this ('smash the patriarchy').

How do we intervene?

Going back, we need to approach 'structures and functions' in a combined way. Rather than trying to change an 'objective structure' directly, we really should be analysing these questions first:

- Why are the outcomes or functions static or slow changing in the first place?
- Where and when have these functions changed in the past or in other contexts?
- How can we or something else change these static forms of functioning and thus change the 'structures' that have been observed?

To change the structures, then, we need to change the way the person or group differentially gets outcomes for how they act in the world. Marxists and feminists are already doing this with class and gender 'structures', but we can learn from them in the other areas of where 'structures' have become dysfunctional and contextualize them better. Easily said, but difficult to do in many cases (V6.8).

When we 'intervene' on the 'individual' what are we really up against? What are the concrete structures and where do they seep into individual behaviour? More will be said in the next chapters (and for mental health in V6).

References

Barth, F (1987). *Cosmologies in the making: A generative approach to cultural variation in inner New Guinea.* Cambridge, UK: Cambridge University Press.

Bentley, A. F. (1895). The units of investigation in the social sciences. *Annals of the American Academy of Political and Social Sciences, 5,* 915–941.

Bloch, M. (1992). *Prey into hunter: The politics of religious experience.* Cambridge, UK: Cambridge University Press.

Durkheim, E. (1982). *The rules of sociological method.* New York, NY: Simon & Schuster.

Evans-Pritchard, E. E. (1965). *Theories of primitive religion.* Oxford: Clarendon Press.

Everett, D. (2005). Cultural constraints on grammar and cognition in Pirahã: Another look at the design features of human language. *Current Anthropology, 46,* 621–634.

Festinger, L., Riecken, H. W., & Schachter, S. (1956). *When prophecy fails: A social and psychological study of a modern group that predicted the destruction of the world.* New York, NY: Harper & Row.

Firth, R. (1960). The plasticity of myth. *Ethnologia, 2,* 181–188.

Fromene, R., & Guerin, B. (2014). Talking to Australian Indigenous clients with borderline personality disorder labels: Finding the context behind the diagnosis. *Psychological Record, 64,* 569–579.

Geertz, C. (1973). *The interpretation of cultures.* New York, NY: Basic Books.

Gerth, H., & Mills, C. W. (1953). *Character and social structure: The psychology of social institutions.* New York, NY: Harcourt, Brace & Company.

Guerin, B. (1994). *Analyzing social behavior: Behavior analysis and the social sciences*. Reno, NV: Context Press.

Guerin, B. (1997). Social contexts for communication: Communicative power as past and present social consequences. In J. Owen (Ed.), *Context and communication behavior* (pp. 133–179). Reno, NV: Context Press.

Guerin, B. (2001). Individuals as social relationships: 18 ways that acting alone can be thought of as social behavior. *Review of General Psychology, 5*, 406–428.

Guerin, B. (2004). *Handbook for analyzing the social strategies of everyday life*. Reno, NV: Context Press.

Guerin, B. (2016a). Arthur F. Bentley's early writings: His relevance to behavior analysis, contemporary psychology and the social sciences. *Revista Perspectivas em Análise do Comportamento, 7*, 1–35.

Guerin, B. (2016b). *How to rethink human behavior: A practical guide to social contextual analysis*. London: Routledge.

Guerin, B. (2016c). *How to rethink psychology: New metaphors for understanding people and their behavior*. London: Routledge.

Guerin, B. (2018). The use of participatory and non-experimental research methods in behavior analysis. *Revista Perspectivas em Anályse Comportamento, 9*, 248–264.

Guerin, B., Leugi, G. B., & Thain, A. (2018). Attempting to overcome problems shared by both qualitative and quantitative methodologies: Two hybrid procedures to encourage diverse research. *Australian Community Psychologist, 29*, 74–90.

Gumplowicz, L. (1885/1980). *Outlines of sociology*. New Brunswick, NJ: Transaction Books.

Harrison, S. (1992). Ritual as intellectual property. *Man, 27*, 225–244.

Kolig, E. (1984). The mobility of aboriginal religion. In M. Charlesworth, H. Morphy, D. Bell, & K. Maddock (Eds.), *Religion in aboriginal Australia* (pp. 391–416). Brisbane: University of Queensland Press.

Leach, E. R. (1954). *Political systems of highland Burma: A study of Kachin social structure*. London: G. Bell & Sons.

McDougall, W. (1923). *An outline of psychology*. London: Methuen.

Mills, C. W. (1959). *The sociological imagination*. Oxford: Oxford University Press.

Rappaport, R. A. (1984). *Pigs for the ancestors: Ritual in the ecology of a New Guinea people*. London: Yale University Press.

Skinner, B. F. (1935). The generic nature of the concepts of stimulus and response. *Journal of General Psychology, 12*, 40–65.

Strecker, I. (1988). *The social practice of symbolization: An anthropological analysis*. London: Athlone Press.

Wilson, B. R. (1969). A typology of sects. In R. Robertson (Ed.), *Sociology of religion* (pp. 361–383). Harmondsworth, UK Penguin.

3 The societal ecologies of modern life *are* our 'psychology'

When ecologists study animals (and even plants) they look for the resources needed by the organisms, the resources available in the location, how those resources are structured in the environment, the ways in which the animals obtain those resources, the other animals cooperating, predating, or ignoring those being directly studied, the climate, the social structure of the animal group, etc. Social anthropologists do similar but with more specialized contextual analyses for humans. In the classic ethnographies these analyses were done in remote locations with people who had little contact with 'modern' societies although this has now changed. The research methods used in both cases also reflect the contextualization needed to understand the organisms under investigation.

As we saw in V4.1, when psychologists in the 1880s wished to understand human behaviour they did the opposite of what ecologists do—and took the opposite path (Pathway 1). Psychologists, and this includes both the Wundtian and the Freudian traditions, immediately disregarded most of the life contexts and looked for answers in the brain, or in theoretical models of what might be going on in the brain. This made a huge number of assumptions, including that there is an unchanging 'processing' structure inside the brain that is constant whatever the environment (Guerin, 2016b; see also V4.8).

While we know a lot from social anthropological research about the ecologies or contexts that shape human behaviours in isolated communities (resources and social relationships directly shaping each other), we do not know so much about the *natural ecologies of modern humans*. That is what this chapter is about, drawing heavily on sociology and my summaries of a lot of social science research (Guerin, 2004, 2016a).

Of importance here are not only the fundamental differences in ecology between the two groups, but also, and of more importance, that these differences still only arise in both groups from the ecologies of (1) resource production and distribution and (2) forms of social relationships that arise from within these contexts. It is not that one is natural and one is modern—they are both natural, but much of our current ecology would not exist without humans changing the world in new ways—both the resource production and distribution and the forms of social relationships. All the good, bad, and ugly of Western societies are extensions of these differences.

How can we link people's actions, talking, and thinking to the large societal contexts?

We start with people needing (1) *the resources to survive and prosper*. If there is any foundational basis for life, resources are the basis for everything that follows. There must be ways of producing or getting resources. But the majority of ways we behave now are no longer *directly* shaped by this, since very few people in modernity directly produce and distribute their own resources anymore, either as individuals or as families.

In *conjunction* with the above, resources for humans have always come (2) *through people*. Solitary roaming humans have been rare in history (unlike felines, for example). This means that hand in hand with resources, we have *needed* to have social relationships and therefore ways of organizing or governing groups of people for resource production and distribution. In traditional groups, people worked as large or small family-communities to get their resources, whereas now very few of us deal directly with resource production for ourselves or our families. We generally buy our food rather than grow it, and buy our cars rather than make them. We no longer get them through our families either.

All this really is about *economics*, which is just a fancy term for *how resources are produced and distributed by people and groups*. In these terms, most of us now have little to do with resource production and distribution. We no longer grow our food, make our things, or exchange our food within families. Formerly, production was done by family-based communities and then distributed through social networks in many different ways described contextually by social anthropologists. Now we have shops and shopping malls to get our stuff and we generally have little idea how the goods arrived at these places or which resources go to which places.

We must treat this all as just observations rather than wondering which is better or worse—there are good things about our systems and bad things, and things were not all better in the old days. Each system of resource production and distribution (economics) arises under certain conditions and shapes different human behaviours. Any system can be really bad for individuals or groups of people. This is not just applicable to our current economic system (both the way that capitalism is forcing the rest of the world to use this model of resource production and distribution, and the current attempts to change capitalism). Remember that many of the 'traditional' family-community groups just died out, they were not utopias (Nordhoff, 1875/1966).

A little bit of quick historical context

Humans have invented a huge number of ways of doing resource production and distribution, depending on the environment, population size, and how easily the resources are available. Social anthropologists give many detailed examples of smaller groups, which led to the formation of larger groups. Each different group showed different adaptations and the contextual idea is to describe the minutiae of all their contexts to show how particular systems arose from these (see, for example, Johnson & Earle, 1987; Scott, 2018). Some did not work, and those communities disappeared (Nordhoff, 1875/1966). If we were put into those same contexts, we would end up doing something vaguely similar or disappear.

In general, though:

- *Resources* depend on environmental availability or the artificial production of resources through working with groups and with human inventions.
- *Social relationships* are partly shaped by how we can get more resources by being in groups, and partly on how we distribute them (this includes social relationships both of cooperative family groups, strangers whom we pay, and historically slaves).

All this is saying is that for contextual analysis you need to know (1) all the contexts for resource production and distribution, and (2) the social relationships for the resource production and distribution to happen (unless you are a solitary person living completely off the land). This is why it is best for analyses to try and record *resource–social relationship pathways* (identical to the social relations of production, see Chapter 6). The two always need to be linked and this can prevent some confusion (see Box 3.1). We have relationships through getting resources and we get resources through having relationships.

Box 3.1 Two common properties of social behaviour that can confuse contextual analyses

There are two other key properties that go through everything in human history and in current life, which can confuse our analyses. They look very different in different types of societies, but they have always made contextual analyses difficult, and they often make human social behaviours look strange:

- Once people are cooperating together for resources, *any way* of keeping the group together will also be shaped, because, as I have stressed, resources and social relationships always go together for humans. That is, there are ways of strengthening social relationships *that do not directly involve resources as immediate outcomes*, and can even seem to waste them, but by maintaining the social relationships these behaviours do help with resources indirectly (e.g. rituals, joking, entertainment, chatting, telling stories, doing even trivial things together).
- Some of our resources and our resource distribution can therefore become important *exclusively* for keeping the social relationships going. That is, there are some things and events that look like resource production or distribution but might function only to keep relationships going. Again, if they do manage to hold the social relationships together then they are in fact indirectly contributing to resources (e.g. shells (Malinowski), bling, dress style, parties, honour, badges, potlatches).

These two are called *cultural practices* and include the use of language as a key learned behaviour for achieving them (V2.7). The crucial point to learn is that the behaviours themselves do not appear to be important for resourcing, so they can look strange—but they are functioning to keep the social relationships working and this indirectly helps resource production and distribution. In fact, some of these only look strange because we can see nothing productive (resources) coming out of them. But that means you have not looked hard enough to find out how they are *really* functioning, and that you need research methods from social anthropology (Guerin, Luegi, & Thain, 2018).

Some social properties of early forms of resource distribution and social relationships (economics)

Early forms of resource production and distribution had particular social properties that shaped human behaviour, but most of these are now unfamiliar to us in modernity. These included:

- generosity modes of resource distribution (just giving people stuff, but reciprocity was expected in the long term);
- sharing modes of exchange;
- some bartering and 'buying and selling' (but not necessarily with money);
- stealing and 'demand sharing' (not stealing in our modern sense because you are entitled to it);
- borrowing;
- inheriting.

While the monopoly of money has banished most of these forms of economics and taken over now as almost the only way to produce and distribute resources among people (and the main way to hold most of our relationships together), you need to learn that there are other ways possible (and we might need these in the future). But you also need to recognize (and study) that there are specific contexts required for these to work at all. You cannot just start up a new community that *shares* everything, since many other conditions need to be in place for any sharing economy to work. Indeed, without large and highly interconnected family groups these might not be possible. Sadly, in the near future we might need new forms of exchange when capitalism fails, so we need to know how to get these to work.

Social anthropologists have studied and compared different forms of social groups and resource production and distribution, and how these shape each other and have been shaped by the resource environments (Rappaport, 1984). For example, with hunting and gathering groups, if the population increases you need to try and restrict the population or else find new ways to get more resources. Historically, the alternatives usually meant growing crops and herding animals but once you do that, the dynamics of the social group will be reshaped or the group will fail. The two go together. *Sedentary existence and growing resources* mean that:

- People interact more (with both good and bad consequences).
- It is more difficult to avoid people and it is more difficult to monitor what people are doing.
- People compete for resources more.

- Fixed dwellings are needed so placement and maintenance of housing requires attention.
- People need to keep cooperating (hunters and gatherers can split groups more easily than sedentary groups).
- Rituals are needed to keep groups cooperating.
- Storage is needed and ways of protecting from stealing.
- Inheritance needs to be dealt with.
- Leaders are needed depending upon the size of the population.
- Ways of managing potential violence become necessary.

What social anthropologists have found is that while there are a few overarching generalizations that can be made, all these sorts of properties are slightly different in different goups. To learn this all properly, therefore, you need to read many different contextual accounts of different groups and see how changes in context concomitantly change the social organization and structure.

The key message from all this is that our behaviour is shaped by the methods of resourorce production and distribution, and the social relationships that follow from these and shape them in turn. This is why when exploring contextual analyses of humans, you need to consider all of these. This is also why you need to be tracing the resource–social relationship pathways for individual behaviours and not just the two independently.

What happened next in human history? The rise of modernity

The bigger 'systems' within which we *now* live were not invented overnight intentionally by a group of people, even if some groups got advantages from them: the rich did not all get together and invent capitalism; males did not get together and invent patriarchy. These systems all came about gradually; some changes were brought about perhaps with good intentions originally, others with definite bad or selfish intentions of exploitation (slavery), but probably most came from inaction and not thinking ahead, or not thinking in terms of the bigger picture. Someone got an advantage (the rich, men, colonists) and they did not think about what this was going to do to other people's lives, although sometimes in history they *did* know but went ahead anyway (like colonization and slavery). There were many previous empires in which large systems of resource distribution were developed and some specific groups became advantaged (Romans, Ottomans, Mongolian, etc.). But none of these involved quite the same systems we currently have, so we are learning the consequences as we go (although the Chinese did have an amazingly large bureaucratic system in the seventeenth century; see Chirot, 1994).

The rise of our current systems—*which have shaped most of your own behaviour remember*—is fascinating and should be studied if you wish to understand yourself, ironically. Part of the *discourse* (ideology) of our current world is that people are free and independent and build their own lives however they want. A quick look at history shows how wrong this is. This is because such discourses are *part* of our current systems and benefit those who do well from our systems and stop everyone else from complaining (see Chapter 5).

I will now go through some of the systems of our modern contexts but will leave out the historical bits in the middle—how we got from small family-cooperative communities producing their own resources while sharing or trading with other small groups, to the conglomerate of societal systems in which you and I are embedded now, and that shape our behaviour—good and bad. I urge you to study these bits in the middle (how things changed over time), because another strong *discourse* (ideology) of our times is that our current way of living is the *only* or the *best* way to live. You need to see that this is not true, despite many positive features of our modern systems of living (at least for some people).

What are our current life contexts that shape our actions, talking, and thinking?

It is difficult to tell which came first, or whether both happened together, but our distribution of resources and our social relationships have both changed hugely from bygone eras. Both are nothing like they were, and the way we are now is unique in history. In the broadest and most impactful way, *our real-life worlds now consist predominantly of getting resources through money and having most social relationships with strangers*. This is 99 per cent of our lives—strangers and money. These are still just resource production and distribution and social relationships, that much has not changed, but they are very, very different, and affect us in very different ways. *Such a situation has never occurred before in human history*. Here are some of the broad changes from previous times in human history.

Our resource production and distribution no longer happen through either people we know or in locations that we know. Our resources get moved long distances and via people we will never know and *whose only obligations to us is through monetary and legal contracts*. Resource distribution is also huge because of the large population of the earth, and there are major issues for both where the future resources will come from and what damage will be done to people and to the environment (Klare, 2012). Also, while we still require or want a variety of resources in life, almost all of these are obtained through a single form of exchange social behaviour—money. This overly narrow focus in life has changed our other social behaviours markedly as well.

Our social relationships have also now hugely changed in that most people we deal with in life (*especially* for our resources) are not kin and in most cases, this means that we do not really know them at all and they have no obligation or responsibility for us beyond their contracts. Many of these people we will never meet (do you know who grows your bananas or who processed your bank form?) and most of the others in the systems we might know only loosely as strangers or as stranger/acquaintances (do you know the people who sell you bananas and can you chat to them about your family?). For other parts of our lives, we have close friends (non-kin) and our immediate nuclear family, but these now have little to do with our resource production or distribution. In these modern systems, larger kin-based families (communities) are very difficult to maintain so many have disappeared. We have few resource exchanges now between people except through money (see Box 3.2).

Box 3.2 What brought about the changes in modernity?

- The *population increase* (because humans were so much better at getting and storing resources than other animals) and therefore from having to deal with so many people, and from resources getting more and more difficult to obtain for larger numbers of people (one of the reasons for colonization).
- The *gradual increase in the use of money* (with all its social properties) and the gradual placement of a capitalist scaffold on our resource production and distribution, which in turn arose in part from the greater population—strangers now grow and distribute our food and goods so food security is an issue.
- The *greater spatial mixing of strangers*, rather than a kin-based group living closely together.
- The *increase in using the word- or rule-based systems* (see Chapter 1) that were needed to organize both larger populations of interacting strangers and larger resource distribution chains, where words or rules were backed up by force and used to manage the systems that had already been in place and the new ones that emerged; our life systems could no longer be organized through family structures and mutual obligations as they once had.
- It is unclear which of the above or all of them led to this, but our social relationships became *focused more on the strangers* who were distributing necessary resources for money and less on the family, who were no longer involved in this.

What are these systems that shape our behaviours now?

All the different forms of life and relationships have different social properties (see Table 3.1). Social anthropologists trace how behaviour is shaped for smaller, isolated communities. But these all began to change as the population increased and the new societal systems arose. This does not just affect the society as a whole but all the individuals within those societies and shapes how they act, talk, and think. These societal changes affect all of our 'personal' behaviours.

In other words, these new societal systems that shape us *are our 'psychology'*. Our 'psychology' is our social and economic context.

To recap, the earlier forms of human life and behaviour were shaped by:

- having to maintain smaller, extended family groups or communities (rather than a 'society');
- being able to work together to get resources directly by cooperation;
- being able to trade with other family-community groups for resources you could not produce (intermarriage was one way of helping this).

By contrast, our Western life goals and behaviour are now:

- working for or with strangers to get money to get resources, *your work no longer directly produces your own resources* (Marx);
- learning how to maintain good relationships with *strangers* to keep that job and to buy your resources;
- dealing with the societal systems that have been constructed in order to manage a large population of strangers all interacting, since this produces more conflict.

(Note that family and non-work-related friends are still present in modern life but they generally no longer link directly to resources, so they have become less important in economic terms and less time is spent with them compared to in kin-based communities. The research question is: what do we still get from family and non-work-related friends now in modernity?)

From society to individual behaviour

The real question now for this book is how do these modern social and societal systems shape our own 'individual' behaviour?

The first basic consequences

Changes in *resource production* mean that most production is only done by a small percentage of the population. Agribusiness means even less so. Most people currently lack the knowledge to produce their own resources and are fully dependent on money to get these (one reason we are not 'free'). Small or community vegetable gardens are probably the most common exceptions, but these currently make up only a small proportion of people's resources. Most of the places where people now live could not support much resource production in any case, so people would have to move.

Those producing our resources do so for money (ironically, to buy their own resources). They range from farms producing food to large manufacturing plants constructing goods and that are run for commercial (capitalist) interests. This in turn means that for those people to do well they must be concerned with selling as much as possible for a profit rather than helping the interests and values of those people purchasing their goods and food. *This is the structure of the world that shapes us*, not a value judgement on those particular producers, who are also living in these systems and trying to survive.

Changes in *resource distribution* mean that this is also done for money, so how, when, and to whom resources are distributed become a question also of profit now (and therefore social influence and stratification). Those doing resource distribution must also gain money rather than help the interests and values of those people purchasing goods and food.

Social relationships need to be thought about as exchanges (resource–social relationship pathways) and not sentiment, so we must always include contractual or stranger relationships since these are real, frequent, and are the focus of our main exchanges now (and our main problems). Changes in *social relationships* necessitate large changes in what people can and cannot do with each other anymore since they no longer have any obligations to or responsibility for each other, other than contractual.

The specific systems built in order to manage large populations of strangers: welcome to your jungle

As the resource production and distribution changed and social relationships changed in association, egged on by growing populations, all our resources became available through a single social exchange—money. So, our relationships primarily became stranger or contractual ones, meaning that there were no community- or family-based obligations, responsibilities, accountability, or monitoring left in place to keep people in check, and there were now more and more people.

This inevitably meant that *groups of strangers* formed (strategized) different ways to protect their resources and their populations producing those resources. From this situation, the large societal systems came to be, and these later got tightly linked to *nations* or *states* (yes, it was not always like this, nor does it have to be). In name and professed goals, these 'countries' protected all of those strangers living in their constructed jurisdiction, but in reality, because they are actually based on resource production and distribution, and on contractual relationships (non-sentimental), they become biased to those with the most money.

We now have these sorts of systems, enforced through nation states:

- *Capitalist systems* of resource production and distribution (and social relationships) control a lot of our behaviour and greatly affect our resource–social relationship pathways (formerly known as our 'psychology').
- *Inequality of resource distribution systems* from having large populations, which affects many people and arises from strangers controlling resource production and distribution, so that who gets what is no longer under the control of individuals and gets stratified. This means a big dependency on strangers for resources.
- Linked to changes in resource production and distribution, stranger relationships, and the large population, *a societal system of marketing run by strangers* directs people to all the options of resources and their distribution, but this is aimed solely at profit making since those people need to get their own resources from what they make.
- *Opportunity structured systems* also arise from strangers controlling or stratifying what opportunities there are in modern societies to get jobs, get access to resources, etc. These are clearly seen in societal systems (such as economic, policing, legal) that advantage groups based on race, gender, 'class', wealth, etc.
- *Legal structures and policing systems* are required not only because of the large size of the populations now, but also because these populations consist of mostly strangers who have no alternative methods of settling conflicts and disputes. Your family has no power to settle disputes with strangers in your life and neither do your local communities of strangers (these two were formerly widespread and powerful systems of governance).
- The *modern patriarchal systems* of male advantages are built into many parts of life, and shape both male and female behaviours but differently. In the modern Western world, patriarchal systems now stem from

male strangers rather than from family members, which has changed the story for us. Because families do not shape the differential gendered behaviours now as much as strangers, it is more difficult to observe these concrete shaping events.
- *Colonization systems* affect us because descendants of the colonizers had advantages built into many parts of life, perhaps without even knowing. As well, all colonized people still have big disadvantages, and these are built into the systems themselves as they were created over the last few centuries, through subtle stratifications of opportunities.
- *Bureaucratic systems and all the traces called modernity or neo-liberalism* (word-based or rule-based organizing of populations) affect us. Because of the large populations of strangers in Western countries, our worlds have become based on written words and rules backed up by the forces of other systems. There are many of these, but everything needs to be checked with written rules before proceeding, since there are forces that will punish otherwise (cf. Chapter 1).

And so, just like social anthropologists mapping how the ecology of jungles structure the resources and living for the communities whom they research, the above form our very own Western jungles, from which we must gain resources and build social relationships. These structures shape our living and our whole lives now.

Once these bigger systems were in place, they had many social properties that determined, through resources or else by limitations of opportunities, all of the 'individual' actions, talking, and thinking of people. We act within these systems of provisions and limitations. So, this is how you should think about the larger systems determining 'individual' behaviour, talking, and thought. And this is how we should now think about our 'psychology', which is merged in the social sciences.

Just like our ancestors in the deserts and jungles, *we engage with our environments to get our resources and we cooperate alongside other humans to do this*. The thing is that what I have too briefly sketched above is now our environment. *Our lives and our 'psychology' are now about exchanging money for resources produced by other people within a large population of strangers*. We cannot get our resources and social relationships except by working through these systems and they are backed by force (bureaucracies, police, army, etc.). All the land in the world is now 'owned' through these systems (nation states), so you still need to work with these systems even if you want to start something new or find an alternative.

How are we affected by these systems?

The aim of this section is to get you to observe and analyse the way societal systems actually shape our individual behaviours, which I will do through presenting a series of tables.

Social relationships

Table 3.1 presents a series of properties that occur for social relationships, and shows how these differ for the different types of social relationships we have in life. Remember that for most people reading this, the majority of your relationships will be in the far right column, and some in the middle. These are just guiding ideas and any real cases you observe and analyse will vary and have exceptions. But if you know the relationships, these can help guide you to look for social behaviours and find the exceptions and their contexts. These are areas to explore with people you are working with rather than 'facts' for all cases or prescriptions. And for those of you who begin working with people in kin-based communities, study the second column really well; this will give you a starting place even though all groups vary.

Economics and resource distribution

Table 3.2 focuses on the Western system of resource production and distribution, which is capitalist. This requires continual growth to maintain, and each person or group along the chain needs to profit.

Bureaucratic neoliberalism

Governing large groups of people has many problems and here the focus is on Western neoliberal bureaucracies as the solution (Graeber, 2015), but other solutions have existed and had other problems (Balazs, 1964; Chirot, 1994; Sutherland, 1979). The way governing large groups of strangers is handled is through using the same verbal, written contractual relations, but in a standard formal way using systems of written rules (see Chapter 1 and V4.7) with the police and army as forces to back up the written rules. The most formal ones are through bureaucracies and the services that run our lives through governments.

We basically have a large part of our lives and futures put into the hands of people we do not know and who have no obligations to us personally, who are following written rules that are supposed to cover all the exigencies of our lives and guide us (V4.7). Every little facet of life is put into verbal rules that are followed (more or less). A major assumption, in fact, is that we can actually document all of life into a verbal system or rules, and that these rules do not just favour some people.

What this means is that a major group of people running our lives (government, work organizations) are merely following written, abstract rules and end up treating us all in an impersonal way. They do not know us at all, and how well we are treated and helped with our problems *depends on how well these rules have been written and thought through*. Clearly, these systems are asking for things to go wrong (Graeber, 2015; V4.7).

This also adds to the increase in language use over other forms of interaction in everyday life, which as we saw earlier comes from capitalism directly. So there is a lot of added conflict and stress in life that is generated through these impersonal forms of running people's lives.

These bureaucracies are a large part of everyday life in modernity, because your resources are coming through these systems, since they include rules or employment and organizations of all sorts—even non-governmental organizations and communities need to follow rules. Resources are distributed and made available in the first place only through impersonal, stranger relationships based on written rules over which we have little control and with whom we have no other connections by family or friends by which we might influence or control this distribution. We now act with respect to a generalized other of society rather than specific family members or community authorities as before.

Hence, a major source of stress and conflict in modernity comes through the bureaucratic and organizational systems run by strangers for our benefit but using written, abstract rules—neoliberalism (Graeber, 2015; Lem, 1973; V6.7).

For the stranger relationships, there is little real obligation or monitoring between those involved; that is, a property of strangers and acquaintances is that they frequently do not have contact among each other—your friends do not necessarily know your family well and your work place acquaintances with whom you spend so much time are often unlikely to mix with your friends and family either. And even the different branches of bureaucracy do not have strong contact between them.

So, surviving rules used for governance by large groups of strangers is another part of the modern jungle that we must navigate. It is now part of our 'psychology' since it plays a huge part in shaping our behaviour and is a skill that must be taught early in life. Table 3.3 lists some of the social properties of bureaucracies that shape human behaviours. If you go through these properties and think of human history, this is a very unusual and strange set of social behaviours we have ended up with.

Table 3.1 Social properties found in three different types of social relationship

Some social properties of relationships	Kin-based or extended family communities	Nuclear family and casual friends	Modern stranger or contractual relationships
Resources exchanged	Almost everything is exchanged within the group, and many life resources can be obtained through the group	A variety of sharing and reciprocal acts, long term with family in some cases, but less so with friends	Through money or a few favours without any long-term commitment, short-term emergencies
Important populations/audiences	All family members related distantly and important Familiar with whole communities in most cases	Nuclear family but less so for cousins and others Friends might not know families and friends of friends might not be well known either	Very little beyond the person or group if it is a work group of some sort Most do not know family or non-work friends
Resource–social relationship pathways	A lot of life resources, including work and financial matters, will come through extended family via family obligations	Family are now limited in providing most resources except companionship and listening as an audience Some family ties might be useful but not regular contact Friends potentially stretch the potential for strong and weak network ties	Strangers now provide most life resources (with money to reciprocate) Being able to deal and negotiate with strangers is a vital skill to fit in with modern life
Knowledge of your other relationships	Family will know most people in your life, they will know the families of your friends, possibly before you were born	Family and friends often do not know each other well, although there are plenty of exceptions. Most only know the work-related strangers in your life from what you tell them, not directly	Apart from work-related strangers, most others have no idea about your family and friends

The societal ecologies of modern life   63

Secrecy and openness	Most things are known to everyone or to groups within Little kept secret Special strategies develop if secrets 'need' to be kept Often distrust of anyone keeping secrets	Nuclear family secrets often kept from wider family Secrets from friends are easy because all are compartmentalized into different arenas of life and they do not see each other often or at all (friends, family, friends of friends)	Easy to keep secrets because very compartmentalized over life arenas Most details related to contract are kept in some bureaucratic form so very easy to find out. Who controls the bureaucracy therefore has some power
Monitoring	Will see most of the people regularly, and the others will see each other regularly so there is much mixing of events and information	Will see some of the people regularly, but not others. The others will not all see each other regularly, except if family perhaps	Will often not see them again, and others will not see each other (e.g. your family probably sees and knows very few of the strangers you deal with in life)
Interdependencies	Everyone depends on everyone, or within subgroups in the bigger community	You are interdependent with family and friends in the limited domains of life where you exchange	Interdependent for contractual part of relationship Few obligations or interdependency otherwise Discouraged in many cases
Reciprocity	Tend to be taken for granted obligations that are not questioned often; not onerous because the same is reciprocated	Usually there are specific supports that are returned in some way, but these vary	Exchange within a society of strangers is primarily done via money
Having trust	Usually good trust between family members from the many interdependencies	Trust between nuclear family members and between friends usually conditional on conditions relevant to their history	Trust weak and dependent upon contractual relations and the ability to enforce the contractual relations. Trust outside of that usually weak

(*continued*)

Table 3.1 Cont.

Some social properties of relationships	Kin-based or extended family communities	Nuclear family and casual friends	Modern stranger or contractual relationships
Ease of escaping or avoiding consequences	Difficult and limited mostly to secrecy and language strategies, or forming coalitions among kin; on the other hand, the family and community will protect from many negative consequences	Only easy if constantly changing networks, if high status within networks, or if there are coalitions within networks (cliques); you can keep things with the smaller groups fairly easily, such as secrets with friends can be kept secret easily from your family	Easy especially if wealthy, and people can easily withdraw from social relationships Secrecy and lying are also easy since you do not usually have to see the persons again
Conforming to common rules or norms with these people	Usually directed towards what the community sees as important and often reflected in historical precedence or ritual practices	Usually directed towards what best friends or closest family perceive is important	Usually directed towards what is publicly available and especially in the media and through government and high-status (rich) citizens
Obligation	Strong kin obligations across almost all activities	Some loose obligations with nuclear families but not with friends Help given is usually only for those areas of life you are involved in together	Obligations follow almost exclusively from the contract, even if unspoken or unwritten If new obligations are sought they will be put into contractual form
Accountability	Through complex family systems with historical context frequently utilized At worst ostracism, which takes away almost all life resources	Through public rules and policing, and through network members' contacts	Mainly through public rule following and policing, institutionalized

The societal ecologies of modern life 65

Reputation/image	Reputation built and utilized within extended family. Most outsiders do not appreciate or take notice of your family reputation	Reputation from nuclear family and what friends say about you. Each compartmentalization in life can in principle have a different reputation or image		Reputation from fulfilling your contractual obligations and little about 'personal' reputation beyond that; only 'personal' reputation if it relates to contract. With strong compartmentalization different reputations can be maintained away from contracts
Self-identity	Based on the wide kin-based family-community. Your identity based on your family and its status or reputation. What you do and say contributes to both	Your identity with family is based on your behaviour and talk within the smaller family or some wider family members, not useful outside of family. Your identity with friends is based on what you do and say, mainly within each friendship group but including reporting things you do outside of that group. Because of compartmentalization you can maintain different identities with different friendship groups and with family		Your identity with strangers can be different as necessary, and is mainly directed at what is needed for the relevant resources in that contractual relationship. Other than that, most people present a generalized 'nice' or polite image to strangers in general, probably because they may be seen by family and friends
How can you influence these people?	Will be important and depend upon the status of the family in the community networks and the person's status within the family. Time spent talking therefore rather than rule following	Will depend upon your status within networks, but because people in your network do not know each and every one else, you will need more verbal persuasion for influence; your family might have little influence in the networks of your friends		Will depend upon having economic (resource) status, often contextualized as a show of commodities

(continued)

Table 3.1 Cont.

Some social properties of relationships	Kin-based or extended family communities	Nuclear family and casual friends	Modern stranger or contractual relationships
What can you get them to do?	Depends heavily upon the family social relationships The same people will be relevant in most arenas of life	Depends upon your networks and the reciprocity you provide The people are usually not relevant in all other arenas of life, so if you go to a gym you might go with a friend but perhaps not, and your family will not be involved in this	Typically by paying someone and can be done at a distance, and in principle there are no other social relationships involved, no other social obligations, does not usually impact on other areas of life
Competitiveness	Competitive within extended families and comparisons often made Multiple interdependencies make pure competition difficult	Perhaps family sibling competition if resource-rich family or lack of other contacts outside Friends might compete for the strongest pathways with others, and this will be reflected in image management Will also depend on whether lack of other friendships in life	Compete for contracts (jobs) since directly tied to all of our resources through money, not just a small part Also strong competition because no other independencies between the people involved, so negative side effects common
Can use influence from your relationship in other arenas of life?	Use other kin or subgroups to help you influence situations	Family and friends only really useful to help you influence situations within the life arenas of your relationships. Outside that they are not much help unless individuals are already important in another arena of life you wish to influence	Strangers not really useful for influence elsewhere in your life, unless by (weak) association of their name (name-dropping)

Helping/altruism	Help usually given to any and all within the kin-based community within the history of the relationships	Helping is conditional or contextual, depends on the parameters of the relationships	Helping in areas of life not connected to contract is discouraged in modern life or even penalized
Types of cultural patterns	Almost everything and anything Widespread but specific to groups, such as clans and kilts, 'national' customs	Family jokes, family-only traditions, nicknames, celebrations like Christmas, (family) in-jokes, nicknames, things not doable in family, regular nights out, repeated planned events together (friends)	Language idioms and colloquial expressions, local customs, changes in word use or pronunciation within a small group, even between strangers, strangers within a smallish group who do not know each other but know the local history and do the same thing (e.g. avoid a place where there was a murder many years ago), languages, religions, governance styles, phatic communication, politeness, and other relationship negotiation styles
Caring for persons over time	Kin-based family usually look after their own, whatever it takes and for however long, although it could be within a subgroup	Nuclear family usually look after each other and for a long time if necessary, typically parents do this for children and spouses for adults Friends usually do not care for friends over a long time if effort and time are needed	Strangers only look after each other over a long time if there is a contract Paid carers, nurses, and hospitals look after people but require payment
Giving special favours	Will do extra because of interdependencies and long history and long future relationships	Families usually do extra for each other because of future relationships, especially parents Friends do favours within limited constraints and usually within the focus of the friendship, rather than in other parts of the friend's life	Depends on extra-contract relationships whether they are needed for smooth operation of contractual relations. Otherwise there is no obligation because of the scope of the contract

68 *The societal ecologies of modern life*

Table 3.2 Social properties of capitalism and behaviours that are shaped when living in capitalism

Some social properties of relationships in capitalism	What these properties shape in our behaviour
Resources exchanged	Most money and exchanges with strangers using that money Strong attempts to create new resources for marketing and selling Strong use of finding markets for distraction and for bonding non-monetary social relationships (entertainments, objects for status, etc.) Marketing of cheap, common goods as it is profitable and there are no social obligations in the contractual relationships
Important populations/audiences	Strengthens stranger relationships and weakens family relationships since few important resource exchanges take place within family anymore Because money (and capital) are dispersed and take place elsewhere, it encourages dispersal of populations
Secrecy and openness	Strengthens competition that then strengthens secrecy
Monitoring	Attention given to money and links to resources and away from family and 'friendship' relationships Strangers in one arena of life cannot usually monitor your other relationships
Exchanges/interdependencies	Primarily through stranger or contractual relationships
Ease of escaping or avoiding consequences	Easier if more money and resources Because capitalism is focused on stranger relationships there are fewer obligations and responsibilities if you escape or avoid consequences
Conforming to common rules or norms with these people	As per any contract, and no formal need beyond that
Obligation	Only obligations for what is contracted between two strangers, and nothing more is necessary
Accountability	Accountability according to contractual relations and held accountable by legal and police services for any violations

Table 3.2 Cont.

Some social properties of relationships in capitalism	What these properties shape in our behaviour
Reputation/image	How much capital you have, and what you can buy; conspicuous consumption therefore important for status
Goals in relationship	To get best (most profitable) contract with strangers
Reciprocity	Activities of goods exchanged for money almost exclusively
How can you influence these people?	Personal influence is through amount of money and building of reputation (also according to money)
What can you get them to do?	For money you can probably get people to do almost anything
Competitiveness	Highly competitive because single sought after resource and strangers have no other obligations to you and vice versa
Knowledge of your other relationships	Within capitalism most relationships do not know about a person's other relationships, unless work related
Can use influence from your other relationships	Within capitalism people cannot usually use one relationship to influence their other relationships, unless some are powerful Stories can be exaggerated more easily in stranger relationships since they do not know each other
Helping/altruism	Little helping outside of contractual obligations
Types of cultural patterns	Superficial and related to contractual activities
Self-identity	Based around contract completions and amount of money/capital
Politeness and deference	Superficial in line with contractual arrangements
Bullying or overriding	Those with capital or money have power to bully since little accountability outside of this
Caring for persons over time	Only if a contractual arrangement
Having trust in them	Trust extends as far as contract indicates, and depends on force used to back up contract (legal, police)
Giving special favours	Little given unless in contract, everything needs to be specified in procedures

Table 3.3 Social properties of bureaucracies and some behaviours that are shaped when living in capitalism

Some social properties of relationships in bureaucracies	What these properties shape in our behaviour
Resources exchanged	Exchange within a society of strangers is primarily done via *money*, but through series of written rules
Important populations/audiences	Bureaucrats are paid to administer rules rather than to help people directly, the intention is that both are done but this depends upon how well the rules can map our lives and situations (V4.7) Informally, bureaucrats can be both better and worse than the rules allow
Secrecy and openness	Bureaucrats are not supposed to go beyond the written rules or discuss exceptions and loopholes to the rules Decision-making within bureaucracies usually kept secret except for the rules that are supposedly being followed
Monitoring	Will often not see them again, and others will not see each other (e.g. your family probably sees and knows very few of the strangers you deal with in life) High turnover so different people, which is not supposed to be a problem since they are enforcing the same rules
Exchanges/interdependencies	No interdependencies allowed with bureaucrats except following the rules No other exchanges allowed with bureaucrats in principle
Ease of escaping or avoiding consequences	Secrecy and lying used to be easy since you do not usually have to see the same persons again, but now there is extensive monitoring of our lives through databases and other means to check on us
Conforming to common rules or norms with these people	In principle this is all that bureaucrats do; if they want to be caring there needs to be a rule about this
Obligation	No obligations beyond the bureaucrat's contract for following rules Personal obligations to people is usually frowned upon since it can lead to inequities in treatment
Accountability	Through public rule following and policing, institutionalized monitoring of what bureaucrats do
Reputation/image	Usually get high reputation if flexible on rules, but the opposite for employers or government who gain promotion by sticking to the rules

Table 3.3 Cont.

Some social properties of relationships in bureaucracies	What these properties shape in our behaviour
Goals in relationship	Following specified rules, and in principle there are no other social relationships involved, no other social obligations, does not usually impact on other areas of life
Reciprocity	No personal reciprocity since the bureaucrat is representing the organization or government and the rules *are* the only reciprocity allowed—what the government rules allow them to do for you—the exchange is through taxes and elections
How can you influence these people?	Will depend upon having economic (resource) status, often contextualized as a show of commodities
What can you get them to do?	Only what is in the rules
Competitiveness	There should be none as everyone is treated the same under the rules; in practice of course this is not so, for example, those with wealth can hire people such as lawyers to wield the rules to their advantage
Knowledge of your other relationships	Bureaucrats will typically not know anything about your family and friends and other parts of your life than those being dealt with; in fact, often different bureaucracies do not know what is going on for the same person
Can use influence from your other relationships?	In principle no, but sometimes this happens; those with wealth can go above the bureaucrats to management and change the rules
Helping/altruism	Only as far as this is specified in the written rules (V4.7)
Refusing to help	In principle this is not allowed unless (once again!) it is specified in the written rules; a bureaucrat must help everyone the same in following the rules unless exceptions are made in those rules
Types of cultural patterns	In principle bureaucracies have fixed and stable social relationships, but in practice different locations and groups develop their own practices that might not be specified in the written rules but are not contradicted

(*continued*)

72 *The societal ecologies of modern life*

Table 3.3 Cont.

Some social properties of relationships in bureaucracies	What these properties shape in our behaviour
Self-identity	The bureaucrat has no presentation to 'clients' except through the written rules. In practice they often do to negotiate the difficult parts of their job, e.g. acting tough to stop people trying to bend the rules, acting nice and "I am so sorry, but I did not write these rules", and acting in ways to make their work more pleasant and efficient
Politeness and deference	Utterly polite except in regard to the rules they are following when they must be firm and not defer to anyone
Bullying or overriding	As above
Caring for persons over time	Will care indefinitely over time but only if this is in the written rules
Having trust in them	In general, there can be trust that the rules will be followed, but those making the rules might not be trusted
Giving special favours	No special favour officially allowed in bureaucratic relationships
Types of humour	Tolerated or frowned upon; the contexts calling for humour require investigation
Apologizing	Only if the rules were not followed, they are not supposed to apologize for the rules themselves
Breaking rules for them	No breaking of rules, that is the whole purpose of this system even when life situations cannot be put into rules

The bigger picture

All the above shape people to stratify, restrict, target opportunities for others, and so we then find major societal systems arising for colonization effects, patriarchy, race, socio-economic status from stratified wealth opportunities, etc. And each of these have produced groups who become lacking in opportunities (through no fault of their own) and discriminated against.

I will not go through details of these since they are covered elsewhere. But if you want to understand 'psychology' you need a good knowledge of these, especially when working with 'mental health' issues (V6.3). You could start with the summaries in Guerin (2016a) but it is better to

The societal ecologies of modern life 73

explore those who were used to construct all this. There is so much more to learn about how individuals are shaped by society that psychology has just ignored (Pathway 1).

To finish, I want to mention Ulrich Beck's version of living in modernity. Ulrich Beck is a sociologist who has also written extensively about the impact on individuals of those societal systems we call neoliberal, but has not been acknowledged in psychology as carrying out the same aim and vision. Here is my summary of what he was saying in his 15 points (Beck, 2000):

- *It is difficult now to have a coherent and unified life pursuing one vision.* The areas of our lives are fragmented and do not interconnect well because social relationships are compartmentalized; this is all structured in our societal systems, not in being disorganized as individuals.
- *The idea of 'individualisms' come from modern societal structures.* We all have to pursue very unique strategies since there is no cohesive whole. Yet at the same time we are all doing this within standardized structures and you are made to be responsible for your own life pathways when you had little choice.
- *The systems of capitalism and bureaucracy force us to become dependent upon them.* Money is a social construction (potentially very flexible) but it is difficult to escape using it within the modern world. Bureaucracies have our lives mapped so we need to stay within those or get punished.
- *Even though our potential biographies are limitless, they have become standardized even when we appear to choose our own.* We all buy the same goods from the same stores.
- *All the above produce anxiety and competitiveness to be actively doing things, being actively individual.* This means that failure in an activity is blamed on the victim and it becomes a personal failure even though all the terms were dictated by the various modern systems.
- *Failure in your life also now appears as your own failure*, even though modern society has already structured most of the parameters of what you can do.
- *The systems are getting more and more unwieldy and so people are finding it harder and harder to work their pathways and are anxious because of this.* With globalization or resource production and distribution we are 'spread' through different geographies in that our compartmentalizations are all over the place.
- *We have no real traditions anymore because stranger relationships break these up.* People are now spending a lot of their time and energy

- inventing new customs and traditions, as discourses mainly, because they have none; these can be familial, nationalistic, or religious.
- *Our lives in modernity can also be characterized as 'experimental'.* There are no certain pathways our forbearers learned that they could pass on to us to help, parents become even less help in negotiating the worlds of their children.
- *Treating people as individuals is seen as a positive thing now, whereas previously it was not—it is a new concept.* Looked at another way, individualism is empty, vacuous, and misleading because we cannot be individuals. We can only do so by pretending that societal systems are not shaping us—a radical form of 'non-identity' that I argue ignores the basics of life, as psychology has done for 150 years.
- *Our lives are pretending to be a lot they are not, in order to pursue capitalist and neoliberal structures.* Often we sense our lives are built on lies and not what we would choose, and in this way many people do not 'fit in' (and may get 'mental health' diagnoses).
- *All these systems are coming into conflict since they are following pathways not related to those living within them*; they are not listening to their members.
- *We are told that we can have any thoughts we want* (even though they come from community discourses), and we are not encouraged to go beyond the systems in place to think about alternatives. Critiquing the social systems becomes inherently discouraged within those systems since you lose so much or get punished.
- *All of the above shape anxiety, depression, or both*, since we are shaped to be individuals creating our own lives and taking responsibility, while at the same time we increasingly do not have control over our lives. Again, many people find they do not 'fit in' anymore.

References

Balazs, E. (1964). *Chinese civilization and bureaucracy*. London: Yale University Press.
Beck, U. (2000). Living your own life in a runaway world: Individualism, globalization and politics. In W. Hutton & A. Giddens (Eds.), *On the edge: Living with global capitalism* (pp. 164–174). London: Vintage.
Chirot, D. (1994). *How societies change*. London: Pine Forge Press.
Graeber, D. (2015). *The utopia of rules: On technology, stupidity, and the secret joys of bureaucracy*. London: Melville House.
Guerin, B. (2004). *Handbook for analyzing the social strategies of everyday life*. Reno, NV: Context Press.

Guerin, B. (2016a). *How to rethink human behavior: A practical guide to social contextual analysis*. London: Routledge.

Guerin, B. (2016b). *How to rethink psychology: New metaphors for understanding people and their behavior*. London: Routledge.

Guerin, B., Leugi, G. B., & Thain, A. (2018). Attempting to overcome problems shared by both qualitative and quantitative methodologies: Two hybrid procedures to encourage diverse research. *Australian Community Psychologist, 29*, 74–90.

Johnson, A. W., & Earle, T. (1987). *The evolution of human society*. Stanford, CA: Stanford University Press.

Klare, M. T. (2012). *The race for what's left: The global scramble for the world's last resources*. New York, NY: Picador.

Lem, S. (1973). *Memoirs found in a bathtub*. New York, NY: Harcourt Brace.

Nordhoff, C. (1875/1966). *The communistic societies of the United States: From personal visit and observation*. New York, NY: Dover.

Rappaport, R. A. (1984). *Pigs for the ancestors*. London: Yale University Press.

Scott, J. C. (2018). *Against the grain: A deep history of the earliest states*. New York, NY: Yale University Press.

Sutherland, H. (1979). *The making of a bureaucratic elite: The colonial transformation of the Javanese Priyayi*. Singapore: Heinemann Educational Books.

4 Contextualizing beliefs as everyday language strategies

The next few chapters take some of the everyday events of life that psychology treats as 'individual' phenomena, and show how they merge with the social sciences, in fact, how they *need* to be merged.

Writing about beliefs as one case of language in context requires following John Blacking's advice: "A musical system should first be analysed not in comparison with other musics, but rather in relation to other social and symbolic systems within the same society" (Blacking, 1995, p. 228). Rather than compare beliefs to other beliefs or to the world itself (are they true, does the person *really* believe them, are they accurate, are they contradictory?), we must analyse them in terms of *what they do within our lives* and within what I call our 'resource–social relationships pathways'. John Blacking is worth keeping in mind throughout this.

The contextual idea is that from the time of birth, our lives are set on getting a wide range of 'needed' resources and this proceeds through social relationships (whether close or familial relationships or stranger relationships), and within the opportunity contexts set by our birth. Every person's resource–social relationships pathways will be different but there will obviously be a lot of similarities and patterns.

In making our resource–social relationship pathways functional, we can potentially utilize any or all of our behaviours and all parts of our environments. As is well known, you can't always get what you want, and in some cases, life becomes dysfunctional and inoperative (some are labelled as 'mental health situations'; see Guerin, 2017 and V6). This is the broad picture of contextual analysis covered briefly (Guerin, 2016a).

Rethinking beliefs

Traditionally, espousing beliefs has usually meant stating a 'fact' about the world and how it works, and is sometimes contrasted with giving *attitudes* and *opinions*. For psychology, we are thought to 'own' or to 'possess' these

Contextualizing beliefs 77

beliefs inside us, and then express or communicate them (Pathway 1, V4). We will see in what follows, however, that these distinctions are about social properties rather than anything more substantive, and that attitudes and opinions are just forms of hedging beliefs.

But if we put all this in context, people's beliefs are just one more behaviour that can have effects in the world to shape our resource–social relationships pathways, in conjunction with all our other behaviours and relationship complexities. Beliefs are *uses of language*, which means that they can only have effects on people and not directly on the world (Guerin, 2016a, V4.3). What effects they have will depend, like any other use of language in life, on the context, the audiences, and the audiences' contexts.

> What were important to the Chinese philosophers, where questions of truth and falsity were not, were the behavioral implications of the statement or belief in question. In other words, the Chinese asked: What kind of behaviour is likely to occur if a person adheres to this belief? Can the statement be interpreted to imply that men should act in a certain way?
>
> (Munro, 1969, p. ix)

So, the broad picture is that in pursuing life's pathways of resources through social relationships we sometimes use the form of language known as beliefs. Put metaphorically, they are like another tool we wield on people in the pursuit of resources through social relationships, although the whole process is much more nuanced and complex than this suggests. But this metaphor might help you get away from the idea that beliefs are 'entities' inside us that we 'possess' and 'process' internally, and that we have computed (perhaps wrongly) from our observations to have a high probability of being true. Instead, talking in the form of 'beliefs' is just a way of doing things to people that has some unique properties (since it has its own label).

Contextualizing beliefs and their social properties or uses

Beliefs are particular ways of talking for managing the social relationships through which our life resources are obtained, just as for any other of our behaviours. The end point of this characterization of beliefs is that we would expect that all the typical properties and events that are found for any human (language) behaviours will also be found for the language use of beliefs. This means we could expect the following:

- Stating "this is the way the world is" (a belief) should be powerful in managing social relationships and resources if the speaker can shape the listener to 'agree' (that is, also espouse the belief or at the least not challenge it). Rather than change the world itself, beliefs can be a way of getting someone to talk about the world in the way you want. But this requires you to have managed the social relationship and reciprocity, not just the belief itself. They are not separable although everyone assumes they are, ever since the 'social' context was pushed out of Western thinking (see Chapter 1).

- Beliefs will depend upon both the resources available and the social relationships. We should expect all the properties of beliefs to work differently, for example, in kin-based relationships and stranger relationships.
- So, what you state as your beliefs are really tools for managing your resources and your social relationships; *ways of doing your social behaviours*. Nothing more. This is a good way in practice (especially for therapists) to understand people stating beliefs. To affect people in different ways with language, we can make a joke, tell a story, ask a favour, or *tell a belief*.
- Beliefs will be wielded or espoused in managing social relationships, that is, in life's melee of cooperation, forming relationships, fighting, exiting of bad situations, etc. People with different forms of conflicts (see Guerin, 2017, Table 4.1; V6) will sometimes use beliefs to change the behaviours of other persons involved but in different ways. Where someone is sure of their resources or social relationships, they can use stated beliefs in effective ways to do things to people, especially preemptively: "Before you say anything, just know that my belief is that … ", followed by an implicit, "Go on, make my day!"
- Even though a person's beliefs are just language and so their material basis is what people do when they hear them, beliefs are likely to be hotly contested in situations of resource limits or in conflicts between those wanting resources. They do not directly change or get any resources by themselves, but they can change other people's access to resources or their cooperation in giving you access. None of what I have said helps us determine which resources or audiences are being contested, that requires detailed observations of any particular case.
- Importantly, a person's beliefs will therefore have *only very indirect relations to their observations and actions* since they are completely shaped *socially* and not by the situations and events they seem to be talking about. Nor are they more strongly shaped by being true. False beliefs can have just the same amount of effects in the world, that is, on the listeners, as do true beliefs, and sometimes even more (since you can exaggerate and warp, and reasonable beliefs are boring for conversation). So, it makes no difference *to the world* whether there

is fake news or true news since all beliefs can ever do is change the behaviour of other people who listen and who have a relevant history. However, if the listeners or readers act on the world after hearing your beliefs then there can be effects on the world, of course, but not directly from the beliefs. This is the problem that occurs when beliefs are said to be 'representations' of the world rather than ways of doing things to people. Philosophers have got this muddled for a long time.

- Your stated beliefs will therefore depend upon the different relationships you have, or more precisely, the different resource–social relationships pathways you have. Some beliefs might be shaped by the immediate groups around you, including friends, family, and strangers (work, etc.), while others will be shaped by broader pathways or pathways from earlier contexts in your life that have not been contradicted (commonly referred to as values but this just means the audiences are more generalized or hidden). Structural groups, such as religions, bureaucracies, and media, will not directly shape beliefs but the people linking you to those structures certainly will. Remember that beliefs are not just shaped purely by these relationships but by the access those relationships give to resources.
- Therefore, beliefs will be a strategic part of most self-image management strategies, face saving, or impression management (along with many other behaviours). If there are compartmentalized relationships, which are more prevalent in modern life, then beliefs will need more management across the different relationships since there might be different beliefs for each relationship and therefore potential problems. This will show up in common strategies of politeness and hedging of beliefs (which includes using 'attitudes' and 'opinions' instead of beliefs), etc. (Guerin, 2003, 2016a).
- For those who say that what they 'believe' does not depend upon pleasing the people around them, but depends on truth, logic, or higher values, they are merely referring to alternative resource–social relationship strategies, which perhaps might have started with earlier groups (such as their family) or have been disguised. For those who say that they 'believe' what they want to believe and have independent or rebellious beliefs, this again is merely an alternative self-image strategy that will be feeding off earlier shaping or current groups in which the shaping is hidden. Remember that "I can believe whatever I want" is itself a belief that is being used in exactly the same way strategically as a pathway. The question to ask is not whether it is true, but what saying this does to those in your social relationships.
- All language use can roughly be functional in two overlapping ways: to get people to do things or to facilitate and manage social relationships

(Guerin, 2016a). With respect to beliefs and the first function, getting people to do things, you will find that the strategic use of stating beliefs to establish social control over listeners in some way is always linked to both resources and social relationships. Importantly, this does not mean that the *content* of the belief has to *superficially match* the resources. If I want someone rich to be buy me a fancy car, I can even begin with the opposite belief: "I don't really like fancy cars, you know. I am not a person who needs to show off with them. But I do think it is important to present a good image … blah blah." You would not negotiate the resource–social relationship pathway by saying: "I want that car and you will buy it for me", unless you already had a strong position in this social relationship. So, *the stated content of the belief itself is not always a good guide to the resources or social relationships involved in the social exchange*, since they are strategic rather than descriptive. You always have to observe how it is functioning in context (why is this person stating this belief in this context?). In a later chapter (V6.6) I will analyse someone stating that their head is a lettuce.

- With respect to beliefs and the second language function, facilitating and managing social relationships, agreeing and elaborating on shared beliefs are common ways of developing and maintaining social relationships, and this is even used by religions and governments for controlling relationships across bigger populations. When making new friendships we often overstate how much our beliefs match. But this is no different to how other forms of language are used to foster relationships (such as humour) or how non-language-use behaviours can do the same (such as sharing a beer or eating food together). Beliefs can be used in the same way. It is the social properties of these different strategies that determine their use—using humour and sharing a beer across very large populations is difficult to pull off, for example, so religions and governments do not use these much.
- Beliefs will function within all the usual contexts: opportunities, economics, historical, cultural, politics, patriarchal, etc. For example, the wealthy in capitalist societies will be able to claim a wide variety of beliefs (even revolutionary) since they can always get their resources through money and without specialized belief strategies—with money you can skip the social niceties (aristocrats were often revolutionaries). But they will frown upon or punish beliefs that seem to go against their way of life, because of both the resource and social relationship implications. The poor in capitalist societies will rarely be in situations in which they can strategically use beliefs in a strong or assertive social way, since they lack the resources or powerful social relationships to back them up. They can state their beliefs loudly and for a long time, but

without the social networks there is nothing to help their beliefs do anything to listeners. They are then forced to rely on non-language forms such as violence or music for getting their resource–social relationships pathways.
- Forming cultural groups does not *have* to involve shared beliefs (Guerin, 2016a, Table 7.1), but, as mentioned earlier, they are often a good way to maintain a group and so will be frequently observed. For example, cultural behaviours such as sharing languages and idiomatic ways of talking probably do not form by sharing beliefs—those speaking Portuguese do not also need to share beliefs. But most religions probably do utilize shared beliefs to hold them together (except some forms of Zen, for example), because other common forms of 'bonding' are difficult to use over large populations (see Chapter 1).
- With this contextual view, any contradictions or conflicts in beliefs are not just uncertainty over what is true about the world. *They are conflicts of social relationships and resources not conflicts of logic* (see Chapter 7, V4.4, and V4.7). As one example, 'cognitive dissonance' is not a conflict over contradictory beliefs (or beliefs and actions) but a conflict of different beliefs for the same person that have been shaped by different, but equally important, audiences—people are stressed about the conflicting social relationships not about the conflicting beliefs themselves. Elsewhere I have shown that the original experiments on 'cognitive dissonance' actually induced these conditions surreptitiously, by the experimenter acting as a new audience and persuading the person to do or say contradictory things without them realizing. It should therefore be called 'social dissonance' (Guerin, 2001, V4.8).
- Beliefs can be restrained, blocked, or punished within some relationships, and there can be beliefs we are not allowed to say with such relationships. Where we have alternative social relationships in our lives, we can hide these 'beliefs' from some of our groups but not others (which is easier in modernity of course). Stating beliefs will be contextual and we can be silent and use other language-use strategies to avoid having to state beliefs out loud for another group of people.
- No one has ever done anything 'because of' a belief. Whatever social negotiations and social dynamic nuances shape us to maintain those beliefs, is also what shapes us to do things.

Exercise

First, think about all your beliefs. This could be in a small domain of your life, or broad beliefs across all facets of your life. Think about beliefs you say out loud and those you never say out loud. Then think about past occasions when you have said a belief out loud, maybe recently, and all the different times you say things you believe out loud. Practice this exercise and then try and notice it *next time* you state a belief out loud.

Now the difficult part. Think about what you did to people by saying these beliefs out loud. How did you want to affect people? What was your expected outcome? What really happened? What were you using your stated beliefs to do to people in each of the cases you remember?

What were you trying to get them to do?

- Agree with you (but what would that do, why do that)?
- Like you?
- Bond with you?
- Stop competing with you?
- Let you guide them?
- Let you dominate them and tell them what they should do?
- Not like you, and distance themselves from you?
- Cooperate with you?
- Make you look good to others?
- Tell you how smart you are?
- Appreciate you more?

Contextualizing how beliefs are changed

It is difficult to rethink how to change someone's beliefs since neither the logic nor the truth of the beliefs are the most important things. Attempting to change someone's beliefs really means that you are asking them to alter some of their social relationships, which can affect their pathways to getting resources for their life, or at the least, changing their beliefs will cause new conflicts in their current social relationships.

- Changing beliefs will be a function of both access to resources in life and our social relationships. If you state new beliefs that contradict those of some of your relationships, then you will need to engage in the usual explanations, avoidance, politeness, hedging, and other language strategies to manage the change (Guerin, 2016a). This is why cult groups take over both the new members' resources and their social relationships (the typical use of *isolation* by cults does both simultaneously).
- As mentioned earlier, if you already have the resources there is no need to change your beliefs or to engage in belief exchanges. At the least, you can engage in stating your beliefs without endangering any of your social relationships. Being consistent is important not for the

- consistent beliefs themselves, but for having consistent resource–social relationships pathways.
- Changing someone's beliefs by merely presenting logical reasoning is likely to fail since beliefs are 'held in place' by the person's resource–social relationship links, not by their logic or by truth. *Trying to change someone beliefs is like a social relationship contest*, not a logical or evidential conflict (see Chapter 1). Changing beliefs is therefore difficult to do except socially, especially if you are not in a social relationship with the person. When therapists try to change clients' beliefs they are wielding their own (stranger) social relationship strategies, not logical persuasion (even for rational emotive therapy).
- I will write more elsewhere about changing beliefs (see Chapters 1 and 7, and also V6), but this rethinking or contextualizing of 'beliefs' is important in clinical work and therapies. It is clinically important in regard to changing the mental health 'symptoms' of *ideés fixes*, disorganized thinking, paranoia, intolerance of uncertainty, delusions, core beliefs, 'cognitive' biases, dysfunctional beliefs, hearing voices, unwanted and intrusive thoughts, grandiose ideas, self-image instability, hypersensitivity to negative evaluation, finding it hard to take minor personal criticisms, feelings of inadequacy, need to control thoughts, perfectionism preoccupation, suicidal thoughts, and body image.

Why it is important to radically rethink beliefs: social and political changes and effects

Contextualizing beliefs changes big issues, involving the wrong ideas of rationalism, thinking controlling action, disengaged cognitions, ideas and concepts, abstracted knowledge, etc. You need to be shocked at the radicality of all this or you have not quite understood.

We do not *have* beliefs; we do not own or possess them. They are just things we hear around us and that we might say, and that can have an effect on people. Nothing more. Our stated beliefs only affect people, even if they appear to be about the world: "If you press this button, the red light will go on". *This statement is a social act*, not an action impinging on the button and light. *Saying 'your beliefs' is therefore always a social and a political act of influence*. In terms of the non-social world, *all* 'beliefs' are therefore fake, abstract, unreal, untrue, disembodied, and virtual. Beliefs do not represent or refer to the world; they cannot be either true or false. They are just actions that can do things to people, and that bit is true and real. Our beliefs do not guide or control what we do, although their *social effects* might end up guiding or controlling what we do (Guerin, 1997, 2016b).

This has all been said before in different ways but the vast magnitude of what this implies needs to be realized. The whole of rationalism, cognition, knowledge, and 'decision-making' are based on false assumptions about beliefs stemming from Pathway 1 (V1.1). The strategic uses of beliefs therefore change with different social relationships and with different resources. In kin-based societies with their idiosyncratic social properties, beliefs can 'belong' to a small group within the community who have the authority and wisdom to say those beliefs (which belong to the whole community). But in line with the social properties, these beliefs must support and maintain the whole community even if invested in a smaller group of elders (usually); they must not just support and maintain the elders themselves.

But in our modern stranger-based relationships we have fragmented and compartmentalized social relationships and resources, so we *appear* to be 'masters' and originators of our own beliefs and to possess them uniquely as individuals. *But this is an illusion* brought about by the nature of social relationships in our current capitalist modern world. The statements we make as 'my own individual beliefs', 'my beliefs and my choices', which we use for our strategic social endeavours, only need to affect our smaller groups of resource–social relationship pathways. Our stated 'beliefs' can remain totally independent of all the other groups in our lives. Unlike the situation with kin-based social relationships, we in the modern world can therefore have different beliefs for our different social relationships. This comes at a great cost, however, in terms of mental health. We are also more likely to 'have' contradictory beliefs to match different social contexts.

This is where the illusion of 'possessing', 'choosing', and 'deciding' to 'have' our very own individually chosen beliefs arises. *But it is a sociological and historical artefact* arising from the different sorts of social relationships and the expulsion of the social from rationality (see Chapter 1). This is also why the whole idea of having our own 'personal psychology' only arose at the turn of the twentieth century.

Examples of language use (stating beliefs) and how this engenders resources

I will say all of what I have said in V4.3, but in a different way and using the language form we call 'beliefs' as my example. The social contextual approach to language use is that is it just a learned behaviour (but a complex one with heaps of training) *shaped to do things to people*. The different forms of language do different things to people or else do them differently. There is nothing more inherent to language than this, and the material basis of language is just a combination of (1) the extensive training we have and (2) the effects we get from other people with the different forms. There is no added meaning, symbolism, expression, communication, representation, or reference to things involved. For the case of 'stating our beliefs', this means that we do not 'have beliefs' or 'possess beliefs', but that we *use beliefs to accomplish our social behaviours*.

We 'do' social relationships for the resource outcomes, not in an exploitative way but in reciprocal relationships of various kinds. *The crux of all human life is doing these resource–social relationship pathways* to get what we and our communities need. These pathways, however, have changed in the last 200–300 years of capitalism from having a small number of resource and obligation reciprocities within large families to having a large number of compartmentalized stranger or contractual relationships in which the parties do not have reciprocal relationships among themselves nor any further obligations beyond the contract.

In order to run our lives and get our resources we therefore need many social behaviours to initiate, facilitate, manage, maintain, and cease our social relationships. Again, these all have very different social properties for kin-based relationships and for stranger or contractual social relationships.

Beliefs therefore enter into our social relationships as do any other social behaviour: through competing, cooperating, bonding, bullying, image management, sharing, agreeing, distancing, reciprocating, hedging, protecting, complaining, controlling, conflicting, being polite, being rude, being humorous, inducing positive and negative emotions, showing off, humbling. You can observe human situations of all these different interactions in which *the stating of beliefs is used instead of other social behaviours* to have the same effect and to get the same resource outcomes.

For example, to bully someone, we might use some form of physical force, we might get others to gang up on them, or *we can bully them with beliefs*. Beliefs are just another social strategy for resource–social relationship pathways. We can do both good and bad things to people with beliefs, and examples of both are given in the following list. Male perpetrators of domestic violence often bully their partners into agreeing with their 'beliefs' about the world. This is done not to help the partner correctly portray the world, but to control all their behaviours (Guerin & Ortolan, 2017).

The following are some examples of how to do some of your social behaviours by stating beliefs:

- *Competing*: trying to get the other person to agree that your belief is 'more true' than theirs. This can be part of a social strategy having *nothing* to do with the beliefs themselves, in just the same way as I can compete with you by buying a better car than yours even though our competition is not actually about cars (it can be about other resource–social relationship pathways). Beliefs can be used in the same way to win resource competitions. With more and more resource–social relationship pathways with the myriad strangers in modernity, it is becoming more and more important to be right. That is, to win 'belief competitions'.

- *Cooperating*: if you want to cooperate with someone, which could be for any number of resource–social relationship pathways, you can go along with their beliefs and add some of your own, which boost your joint agreement.
- *Bonding*: 'collaborative talk' is one form of bonding through telling the same beliefs and agreeing, in this case by telling the beliefs together at the same time.
- *Bullying*: 'talking down' someone's beliefs is bullying, as is also using physical means (interruptions, 'puffing yourself up', talking louder and over the top of the other person, pointing with finger) and social means (using authorities you know or name-dropping) to get agreement with your beliefs.
- *Image management*: presenting images of who you are (who you want to be seen as, that is) by the sorts of beliefs you spout. "Of course, I was most affected as a child by David Attenborough's views on climate change since I have always been a person who believes that we should live with our environment rather than exploit it."
- *Sharing*: sharing often leads to bonding, especially when sharing secrets. Beliefs can be used for this function, and to test and build trust. "I do not normally tell people this, but I believe we are all on earth for a reason."
- *Agreeing*: relationships can be maintained or strengthened by agreeing, and stating beliefs is a common way to do this. Friends often spend a lot of their time together reiterating their agreed upon beliefs that they have repeated to each other many times before. "Yeah, like you have said before Tom, this country's problem is that … "
- *Distancing*: you can use beliefs to break relationships or distance yourself by giving beliefs counter to the other person. This could also be by raising topics (as belief statements) that the person does not want to hear, especially about the relationship. "Looking at us objectively Tom, we have never really been close and there are a dozen reasons why this is true."
- *Reciprocating*: giving beliefs to 'help' another person can be one way of reciprocating obligations. However, care must be taken not to fall into 'controlling'. "I have always found it useful to believe that because we are all born the same then people cannot make me believe things I do not want to believe." People can learn to regard giving beliefs as a gift. This is often seen on social media, even with malice.

- *Hedging*: hedging or modifying the impact of what we do and say to other persons is a key part of managing resource–social relationship pathways. Giving beliefs about events can accomplish this as can many other ways (such as saying you are sorry). "Sorry to be harsh Tom, but I firmly believe that you need a nudge at this point for your own good and believe that this will all work out well."
- *Protecting*: we can protect friends by shielding them or stopping others from hurting them. This can be done using all the strategies given in both ways. "Yes, I know Tom was attacking you but you need to remember that Tom will be in trouble over this so he is going to leave you alone in future. I believe that everyone is on your side in any case."
- *Complaining*: a lot of time is spent by some people complaining, which, ironically, is often done among friends as a potent (negative) way of agreeing, bonding, or cooperating with each other. "Yes, I know, those sorts of people are just bad through and through and I believe that this government should be doing something to stop them because I know that they will keep doing things until the government acts. But our government is totally useless!"
- *Controlling*: words cannot control people without using the balance of resources (power) in the relationships since words themselves have no power (V4.3). Within this, people control others by controlling their beliefs, that is, what they can say and not say. This is clear (and blatant) in abusive relationships where one party bullies the other into agreeing with their worldview (set of beliefs) and not letting them have their own set of beliefs (Guerin & Ortolan, 2017). They are also then indirectly controlling the other persons' audiences and social relationships by doing this.
- *Conflicting*: like competition, conflicts about anything (resources of different types) can be carried out over disputed beliefs even though the beliefs themselves are not the conflict problem. "You are totally wrong, Tom. Not only is your view wrong but you have purposely misunderstood my beliefs."
- *Being polite*: when we talk to certain people, we can be polite in what beliefs we say and how we say them. "Yes, I understand what you are saying about a flat earth, and I believe there are, in fact, some points you made that seem to make a lot of sense."
- *Being rude*: "What you are saying is complete balderdash and only an idiot would not agree with what I stated was my belief."
- *Being humorous*: humour is one of many forms of talk to strengthen social relationships, and what is said is often not as important as *how* it is said. Beliefs can also be made funny in such contexts or by exaggerating them for effects. "Tom believes that capitalism is the best

economic system ever, and it is my belief that he is right, and so we should sell him off to the highest bidder! Haaa haaa."
- *Inducing positive and negative emotions*: like humour, saying beliefs can be emotional in many other ways (V4.6). "This is going to be upsetting probably, I am sorry, but I believe that Tom is going to leave you soon."
- *Showing off*: one form of image management in which you say only those beliefs that make you look good. "Everything I am telling you comes from years of careful study with the best teachers, and I have practised it as well as studying the area meticulously!"
- *Humbling*: "My beliefs are probably all wrong and insignificant", "You will probably think I stupid saying this, but I think that ..."

With all of these examples you should be able to begin noticing all around you the roles of beliefs in managing social relationships and hence resources. As mentioned, some observational research with good descriptions of context (to demonstrate the social functioning more clearly) would be the next step.

References

Blacking, J. (1995). *Music, culture, & experience: Selected papers of John Blacking*. Chicago, IL: University of Chicago Press.

Guerin, B. (1997). How things get done: Socially, non-socially; with words, without words. In L. J. Hayes & P. Ghezzi (Eds.), *Investigations in behavioral epistemology* (pp. 219–235). Reno, NV: Context Press.

Guerin, B. (2001). Replacing catharsis and uncertainty reduction theories with descriptions of the historical and social context. *Review of General Psychology*, 5, 44–61.

Guerin, B. (2003). Language use as social strategy: A review and an analytic framework for the social sciences. *Review of General Psychology*, 7, 251–298.

Guerin, B. (2016a). *How to rethink human behavior: A practical guide to social contextual analysis*. London: Routledge.

Guerin, B. (2016b). *How to rethink psychology: New metaphors for understanding people and their behavior*. London: Routledge.

Guerin, B. (2017). *How to rethink mental illness: The human contexts behind the labels*. London: Routledge.

Guerin, B., & Ortolan, M. O. (2017). Analyzing domestic violence behaviors in their contexts: Violence as a continuation of social strategies by other means. *Behavior and Social Issues*, 26, 5–26.

Munro, D. J. (1969). *The concept of man in early China*. Stanford, CA: Stanford University Press.

5 Self, identity, consciousness, and meaning as social actions in context

Contextualizing the 'self'

> When someone tells me about their self, their self-image, their identity, or how they see themselves, they have already told me all about the social relationships and resources in their world—even when they tell me that they do not have a 'self-image' at all.

There are two parts of self-identity from a contextual analysis: what a person *does*, performs, and has accomplished, and how a person *talks* about themselves (and this includes thinking of course; see V4). These two can potentially have little or nothing to do with one another, but both are intricately bound up in our social and cultural contexts and how we obtain and manage our resource–social relationship pathways. You cannot make up the first, what you have done, but you can make up talking about it—I might never have played sport but can still talk about myself as a 'sportsperson'—however, such fictitious talk still comes from my social and cultural contexts.

This means that most (but not all) about our self or identity is constructed primarily with language use, to portray ourselves in certain ways to gain resources or relationships (or lose resources as well of course). Identity is how we talk to people about ourselves and present ourselves to others, and this will usually include what we have done or accomplished. But this is not done for fun (although it can be fun) but is strategic, to position ourselves for making our lives actually work—to get the resources and social relationships we need or want for ourselves and our families and communities.

Unfortunately, 'self' as an everyday way of talking about ourselves has been appropriated by psychological theories (one of the three responses to Gestalt; V4.1), including Freud's 'ego'. These theories all purport that our inner self or ego *makes us do what we do*, as if it is a cause or a driving force.

Contextually, however, whatever life resource–social relationship pathways have been shaped for us, they have shaped *both* what we do and how we might talk about ourselves. The talking about ourselves does not control what we do. This is why another theme of this chapter is that thinking does not control what we do.

So, there is nothing 'authentically' self in what you *say*, it is all constructed. This just follows from one of the main points of a social contextual approach (V4.3); that all talking and language uses do not have truth or falsity as properties, they are never true or false or authentic. However, the 'self' is not randomly constructed either; it is built from our life contexts and what is available and what needs to be done *and said* to gain resources through people and build a life (Guerin, 2001). If you have not accomplished very much in your life to help build your resource–social relationship links and talk about this, then you will be forced to construct an identity with more fiction added, at risk. While we could make up anything at all about ourselves ("I won four Olympic gold medals once"), identity statements can be checked and monitored so limits are usually drawn as to what can be said. Contextually, this in turn depends upon the sorts of social relationships in which this talk takes place, some will check more than others. Consistency between spoken versions of talking about yourself will become important to check also.

Here are some examples:

- In earlier times and with kin-based communities, your 'identity' came very much automatically from your family and your life position; you were who your family were to a large degree (since they were your resource–social relationship pathways), and people could check very easily. The community knew most of what you had actually done in life irrespective of how you talked about it (most of the community knew of you even before you were born). If they ever let you get away with exaggeration, then that was also part of your social relationships with them (part of a joking relationship).
- Even if the kin-based community shaped a sense of 'individualism' for how a person talked about themselves, this 'self' was fully directed towards the community (Glaskin, 2012; Myers, 1991; Walker, 2013): "I will work hard to make this community strong!" Your talk of an 'individual' self came from your helping the community, not helping yourself alone like modern individualism (Siedentop, 2014).
- When you have those times in life when you are alone and told to 'look inwards' and seek your authentic 'self', remember that all you will find 'inside' are stories, words, and conversations, real or imagined (also like looking in a mirror). Even *remembering* your own experiences or

Self, identity, consciousness, and meaning 91

accomplishments is an experience of words after the event, it is not the original 'doing' anymore (V4.8). This is not a bad thing (unless you take your fantasies too seriously) because in doing this you can explore *new* stories and alternative endings; you can see alternative versions of the past; other possibilities. However, to build a satisfying life and something more than talk and superficialities, you cannot just shape stories about yourself, your past, and your relationships with people. You have to change and shape the world and people, as they do with you, and let your accomplishments in these new worlds you have actually created in turn shape how you talk about yourself.

- If we have a *stable* sense of selfhood that is constant and strong, this is because we have a *stable* environment of resources and social relationships. As will be discussed in this chapter, however, this has been eroded in modernity because we need to build so many relationships with so many strangers who cannot provide stable interconnectedness between all our other social relationships in the way that family and kin-based communities were able to do.
- So frequently changing how you talk about who you are, what you like and dislike, what you believe, etc., is not the fault of young people but of the modern societal contexts we are shaped in (see Chapter 3). The compartmentalization and marketing of life means young people are forced to constantly reconfigure how they talk about themselves to different and new audiences.
- The sense of self also arises from the (false) experience that what we do follows from what we think and say; that our thinking controls our actions (Hodgkiss, 2011). That is, because we have a sense that our thinking controls what we do, this 'thinking' becomes like a strong sense that there must be a 'self' or a 'me' (more on this later in the chapter and also in V4.4).
- This means that if social relationships have been damaged from living in bad life situations (V6.3), then the 'normal' (i.e. social) connections to reality will be loosened as well. The direct sense of 'reality' will not be affected (cf. Bleuler, 1911/1950), and walking around and seeing, and lifting chairs, etc. will be fine. But so much of how we 'put' together reality and then have *to talk about it as reality* is based on having the social relationships for learning all this (called 'social scaffolding' sometimes). Despite being able to lift chairs, doing this action will usually occur under social relationship control and be subject to punishment, evaluation, needing explanations, etc.
- So having a 'disturbed sense of reality' can mean two very different things. Almost all of Bleuler's descriptions of 'schizophrenia', for example, are about talking and discourses and the person showing

only weak control over these. All the 'associations' and 'affectivity' are not connected to reality but this means not connected to the social/discursive ways our realities are 'packaged' in terms of consistency, plans, goals, justifications, self-identity talk, coherence, grammar, etc. Basically, *if bad situations lead to a major loss of social relationships then this will also lead to a major loss of social/discursive reality.* Various symptoms relate to this occurrence, but they are held together by weak social relationships not a brain disease (Scalabrini, Mucci, Esposito, Damiani & Northoff, 2020; V6.4).

The real analysis for self and identity, therefore, lies in observing and documenting the life strategies that engender the statements and actions about self that occur, and when they occur. Hence the opening statement of this chapter.

A contextual analysis for 'self-identity' therefore requires consideration of the following:

- How is it that we need to present at all (mostly through talking but some actions) to gain and maintain social relationships for resources? Why are we talking about a self-identity in the first place?
- The forms and strategies of doing this for the person's specific social and other contexts.
- Economics (resource production and distribution) and identity (especially in modernity; "What line of work are you in?").
- Cultural patterns of identity (different groups shape us to behave in different ways for social relationships resources).
- What we keep secret from our 'identities', and how we then broadcast our version and to whom.
- How we monitor others' identities and use this.

Special features of self in kin-based communities

There are many good studies (mostly in social anthropology) of the 'sense of self', or talking about 'self', in kin-based communities. The broad story is that your 'self' is mostly about your family, your status within the family, your tribe, your clan, your social groups within the community, and a little sometimes about what you do within the community for resources (generalist or specialist?). But in real cases it is much more complicated.

If, as is often the case in social anthropology, your resources come almost solely from community self-sufficiency, then this is indeed where everyone builds their talk about 'self'. Everything to gain resources through social relationships is based around the community, not you as an individual. This also means that specific events that one individual did that is different to most others in the community will be emphasized. But when people have to move from community self-sufficiency to modernity, the details of identity change because the resource–social relationship pathways are so different.

This is a very broad picture and every ethnography shows something different, but you can trace those differences back to resource–social relationship pathways (Glaskin, 2012; Myers, 1991; Walker, 2013).

Special features of self in modernity

In modern Western societies all this has changed (Guerin, 2016). With the advent of modernity in the late 1800s, when the majority of our relationships shifted to strangers (non-kin), *the social properties or logic of identity also changed.*

We now need to build pathways with a lot of strangers who do not know us well, and do not know our families or histories either. This is good because we can make up bits of our 'identity' or exaggerate and they are unlikely to be monitored, but bad because our identities will be multiple and more variable. We will have less chances to check someone else's identity talk and we can then be fooled by people. So, we now need to try harder to convince strangers as to your place in the world and what you can do and what you should receive, but it is also now more difficult for strangers to check what you say about yourself, so you can invent more if you are persuasive. On the other hand, strangers can ignore what you say about yourself or disagree, as there is no network of family to back up what you say—they can ignore you with impunity.

What this really means in modernity is that *we now actually need to spend more time constructing our identities and positions in this modern world*, to get the resource–social relationship pathways we need. This often seems (especially to older generations) like time wasted on paraphernalia, talking about ourselves incessantly, accessorizing, obsessively finding out what others are doing, posting on social media, and constructing stories about ourselves to give other people. So much of our actions, talking, and thinking all now have to go into these sorts of activities: maintaining reputations, personal image management, being up with the latest and the greatest trends, impressing people, keeping up on Facebook, knowing what we should know and a few things no one else does, showing off, finding out about the people around us we do not know just in case they are unsafe, and acting in ways that gain the attention of people who otherwise have no other (i.e. family) interest in you.

In the modern world this can give the impression that we are self-contained and egotistical 'individuals' and that people do not depend or need other people anymore, but this is an illusion. We now need more time to deal with people because most are strangers and compartmentalized in our lives. We are not 'individuals' because we seem distanced from other people and seem to spend less time forming 'close' and stable relationships with people; we seem 'individual' because we all have different, 'unique' contexts. We probably spend more time dealing with our relationships, but in the modern world these are necessary relationships with disconnected strangers (Bhatia & Priya, 2018; Jackson & Holbrook, 1995; Pickren, 2018; Rose, 1996; Teo, 2018; Verdouw, 2017). And because it is frequently unclear what is even required of us to fulfil these goals, since they are strangers we deal with and do not have a lifetime of background interactions with them, this means, in fact, that *we now spend more effort on social relationships than earlier forms of society*, rather than less, but in very different ways.

So, far from being freer of other people and more distant and independent, as modernity strengthens and as kin-based communities lose their influence, we in modernity have probably become far more dependent on other people. But the behaviours that keep us linked with these strangers are more whims and fads and fashions guiding us through multiple stranger relationships, rather than the more direct or obvious resource implications found in closely structured families and communities. Even marriage has, in some ways, become less about your family and more about presenting yourself in a way to convince a stranger and their family to commit their lives (and resources) to you.

With the advent of modernity and the colonization by capitalism of all the things we need in life, we all *need* to do a lot of image presentation and self-identity talk in some form or another. But this is recent and a direct result of capitalism and the changes occurring in modernity with social relationships, not because people have become shallow and more independent of social relationships. The rise of these new self-identity behaviours came about when our resources for life stopped coming through family and was replaced by having to convince strangers about who we are and why we should get what we need (for jobs, reputations, relationships, kudos).

But an even more telling difference, what you have accomplished in life to achieve concrete outcomes—what you have actually done in your life that is good—has become less important than using rhetorical and Internet skills to convince people who you are and what you deserve. Telling a good story is now more important for a sense of 'self' than what you have actually done or accomplished otherwise. Again, this is not because 'young people today' are shallow and self-centred, but because this is shaped when living in the capitalist and neoliberal jungle (see Chapter 3).

Finally, the shift to persuading people of your identity rather than showing it through family/community engagement or through other actions, has meant that those who were privileged in society have even more privilege now. They can afford to present important or personally useful identities. Those who are less privileged (the poor, the oppressed, the less educated) have to give up trying to present identities, or else spend a lot of time on more superficial and cheap ways to make an impression on strangers.

Self-awareness and consciousness

The whole idea of self-awareness or consciousness also changes (V4.4, V4.7). What is called 'self-awareness' is not about a real inner core of authenticity, and this applies equally when *talking about yourself to yourself* (that is, thinking about yourself is shaped by other). Just talking about yourself is not some inner self-awareness, not even when talking as if to yourself about yourself alone in your room.

Talking about yourself, as we saw above, is about influencing your various audiences (social context) to see you in certain ways. And so, thinking about yourself is also just like talking about yourself but not out loud (V4.4). However, just as we saw for talking/thinking (V4.4), once the talking is not said out loud it does have different social properties that make it seem different. This is why our thinking about our self or identity seems to be different from telling people out loud. But this comes only from the social properties (external) of not being said out loud, not because you are digging into 'deeper' inner-self things. In particular (compare Box 4.2 in V4.4):

- If it is thought rather than said then there will be parts of the person's world that have restricted it being said out loud.
- You do not get your 'identity' talk consequated if you are only thinking about your 'self'.
- You will have other talk you have kept secret that people will not know if not said out loud.
- Any exaggerations or fantasy elements you think as part of your identity talk do not have to be checked or monitored.

So, if standing in front of a mirror and trying to plumb the depths of your 'authentic' self-identity and gain true 'self-knowledge' is all wrong, just an exercise in fiction writing and what will convince others if you ever said it out loud, what *is* real about your identity?

Real self-awareness instead would be all about being able to describe the contexts that engender your own actions; being able to describe in detail the various things you do and the thoughts you think, as multifarious, contradictory, and situation-specific as these might be. It would be about describing in detail the historical, social, economic contexts in which you have found yourself in life, and how these strategic contexts link to the various things you do, what you say, and the thoughts you think.

True self-awareness, paradoxically perhaps, requires you going outside and analysing everything you can about your own social, cultural, historical, economic, and opportunity contexts that gave (and will give) shape to all the things you do and think and say, the strategies you have developed through life with people and resources that were available. You would need to do participant observation of yourself (observing and recording systematically what it is that you actually do, say, and think all day and the contexts in which they occur), a lot of time, a lot of questioning, talking to people, reading records, etc. And ironically, you will have to learn much of this 'self-awareness' *from other people*, and from detailed inquiry of externalities, not from navel-gazing and talking about yourself to yourself alone in your room in front of a mirror. If you can do all the above, you will gain true self-knowledge and self-awareness.

What does thinking about 'self' do, and especially thinking about yourself?

As a summary of thinking, we saw that we talk a lot and some of this talk does not get said out loud (V4.4). We also saw that talking (and thinking) are shaped by external situations and from doing things to people with words. We also saw that the things we ask people to do for us, usually get done; not because we or our words have magical powers but because we usually only ask if it is likely to be done or our social relationship gives a context for this. We do not usually ask people to do outlandish things, and need special contextual preparations if we do.

Putting these together and now applying these points to not saying our talk out loud (thinking), we find a novel and somewhat unusual way to think not just about self, but also to those parts of what we call our 'selves' that are *intentions* and *plans*, how our behaviour is controlled. We normally assume that our thinking controls what we do, but this is also just a false appearance. *The 'feeling' that our thinking causes our actions is no different to the 'feeling' that our words alone get people to do things for us.*

Here are the main points again (cf. similar ideas in V4.4, section titled "Why does it feel like 'I am my thoughts' and 'my thoughts control my behaviour'?"):

- All our language use is shaped in our external social contexts.
- We do things in the world and we usually have some talk/thought running 'alongside' (in case we have to explain to someone) but this does not control or cause us to do whatever things they are.

Self, identity, consciousness, and meaning 97

- What we say out loud about what we 'intend' to do most often turns out to be correct but this is only because (like our persuading other people to do things for us) we do not think (talk but not out loud) outlandish things ("I am now going to fly to the moon"), and the thoughts are already shaped by real social contexts; but they do not turn out to be correct because the thoughts have controlled the behaviour.
- This illusion makes us talk about us having an inner self that controls what we do; just as our contextual selection of what we ask people to do for us gives us the illusion that our words or our magical power can get people to do things for us.
- This makes us think that those thoughts, running alongside for later social talk about what we will do anyway, *are* our self or *are* our intentions and that we control all this through *our* 'inner' thinking.
- We get surprised when our talk/thinking does not match what we end up doing (although it was only ever a running commentary in case we needed to say something to someone or explain what we are doing).

As an example, suppose I announce (out loud) in the kitchen, "I am going to the shops to get milk":

- The action of getting the milk has been shaped by external contexts (someone asking you, to make cereal for your dinner, getting away from someone in the house you do not like, etc.).
- Whether you actually do it also depends on external contexts (cannot find shoes, someone interrupts with something else, the person you are getting away from announces that they will come with you if you go to the shops, etc.).
- Your *announcement* that you are going to the shops is a separate event to the later walking bit but only affects people, so it will also be part of your current social situations and negotiations of what you and the people around you are doing.
- Your *announcement* is not shaped by the lack-of-milk external context, because you could just not say anything and go to the shops silently. It is social and might be shaped as a friendly gesture so no one is worried about where you went, to show your independence, a family joke, etc.
- There might also be a possibility that just walking out with no announcement will lead to other problems (e.g. if you had an accident while out), so an excuse or reason is needed in the specific context.
- It could also be that 'going to the shops' is purely part of the same social strategy that led to you talking out loud at all, and you do not actually need milk. If the main context was to get away from someone in the kitchen you do not like, you probably did not even need to announce

it—just walk out of the room and go somewhere else. If you wanted to present your 'self' as independent you might announce going to the shops but then that is enough—you end up not actually going.

But the important point here is that *neither the thinking nor the announcement 'caused' you to leave the room and go to the shops*—the whole social situation shaped the leaving, the talking, and the thinking, but each in different ways.

The constant repetition of scenarios like this in our lives makes it seem (falsely) that *saying what we are going to do causes the behaviour to follow*, that 'we' decide our intentions and then 'we' do them. And remember that it usually does happen that what we say or think of as our intentions (a social event) is what we do (an externally controlled event), but only because we state obvious and common intentions socially. When we state a totally unrealistic intention ("I intend to be king of the world by tomorrow"), it is obvious that this is shaped by the effects this has on other people, but when we state the mundane and then do it ("I am going to the shops" and you go), we now claim that our 'inner' intentions caused us to do it. And this artificially forms the 'me' and the 'I' and the 'self'.

Summary: "why does it feel like 'my thoughts control my behaviour'?"

We have just seen that it is common to experience that our behaviour seems (falsely) controlled by what we think: we think of or say out loud what we will do, and then we do it. The points just listed explain why this is *not* true. But because this experience is very difficult to change, I will elaborate more explicitly. Skip this next section if you understood the idea above okay (it is also given in a different way in V4.4).

When discussing *directives*, asking people to do things for you, it has been pointed out that it seems like words can just magically make other people do things. Most of the time we ask someone to do something, and they do it. "Can you pass the salt please" and hey, presto, it is done! But, we forget that reciprocities in social relationships are needed to make language 'work' and do things to people. It is not the words that are controlling the person but your social relationship histories and reciprocities. However, there are more reasons why it seems like our words automatically get other people to do what we ask of them. For example:

- They were frequently going to do it anyway.
- We tend to only ask people with whom we have an ongoing reciprocal social relationship (which gives the 'power' to our words).

Self, identity, consciousness, and meaning 99

- We tend not to directly ask people to do things if they are unlikely to comply (as related to reciprocities).
- We tend to ask only reasonable requests and not unusual or difficult requests.

Because thinking is just talking but not out loud, we can now apply these same points to our *thinking* as well, *when it appears as if we are 'telling ourselves' what to do next*. Remember that our 'thinking' will really be a discursive commentary *for other people* but not said out loud—justifications, excuses, humour, distractions, etc. So, as we do things in this world we usually have 'running commentaries' on what we do, especially excuses and reasons to give to other people if necessary afterwards.

So the reasons why we have the belief and experience that *our* thoughts are controlling *our* behaviours, follows directly from the above:

- We were always going to do it anyway because of the contexts we are in—whether some talk was thought or not.
- Our 'thinking about something before doing it' only occurs with special things we do, most frequently those that have additional social relationship requirements that might need to be responded to before or after what we are doing.
- Because of the above we hugely *underestimate* how much we do in life *without* any concurrent thinking (because we are not concurrently responding socially in words so we are not aware that we are not thinking about what we are doing).
- We also underestimate occasions on which for *social* engagement we 'promise ourselves' to do something but it never happens; on those (rare) occasions when it does eventuate, the social engagement brings it about not our thinking itself (e.g. "I will stop eating chocolate tomorrow").
- If we are 'thinking' (rather than saying publicly out loud) what we are doing there will be no social consequences because it is not out loud, so there is less likelihood we are controlling our actions with the thinking but it appears even more so.
- So, when we find ourselves talking (not out loud) about what we are doing and what we will do, this 'thinking' is still like a concurrent running commentary for social engagement but is not for getting ourselves to accomplish those tasks. If it helps at all it will be because of social punishment for not doing what we said we would do (Guerin & Foster, 1994; Lloyd, 1994). But this is different when we have not said it out loud so it appears even stronger as if our thoughts control what we do.

- Note that this has huge implications for how we do therapy and how we think about and handle 'thought disorders' (more later in V6).
- Our experiences of 'self-control' and 'willpower' are also based on external social and historical contexts but these are usually hidden and very difficult to observe; they usually involve 'thinking' and so all the above applies.
- In other situations, in which it is obvious that the external environment has shaped what we do, we do not even bother talking about 'willpower' or 'decision-making'. For example, being hungry and *not* eating the delicious food in front of you is talked and thought about as 'willpower', but when hungry and you *do* eat the food given to you, we do not even think about this issue at all. *So, we are selective in the situations in which we even talk about our thoughts controlling our behaviours* (because the first is possibly going to need social excuses and explanations afterwards, but not the second).
- If we try and use 'self-control' this can appear to work because (1) it was going to anyway, (2) there are strong social contexts to do what we say (unless you only 'think' it), (3) you have no excuses or explanations to give if you do not do what you are thinking, and (4) you say your thoughts out loud (to a therapist perhaps).
- If you have thoughts of 'self-control' or 'willpower' but also have thoughts of many excuses or explanations that could work if the behaviour does not happen, you are less likely to do it; so, you need to explore from what external contexts your 'excuses or explanations' thinking/talk arise.
- If you have thinking of 'self-control' or 'willpower' in the first place, you need to explore the contexts from which these also arise; why do you even have these discourses of "I can do this" and "I will do this'? In most contexts of life, we do not engage in such discourses, so what is special here? Punishing audiences?

So, in a similar way to all the above, and to using directives to get people to do things for you, the outcomes of 'telling yourself' to do things depends on your contextual worlds, and mostly social contexts because talking/thinking is involved, but it does not happen directly *because* of the thoughts.

Reasons and meaning

There are two more features of our talking and thinking that sometimes give the (false) experience of an 'inner self'.

Reasons

We have strong experiences that when we do something (or even when we say or think something), that we have *reasons* for doing these. That is, once again, this becomes a (false) experience that our 'inner' reasons are what *make* us do those things, or *controls* us to do those things. This is like we have seen above: it is an illusion of a 'self' but a very understandable one:

- We do not do things because we have reasons.
- Our social and discursive worlds give us the reasons so it only looks as if we follow our own reasons.
- Our external social contexts shape us to talk and think these reasons so we can say them afterwards as excuses, explanations, for making it look like we are responsible for good outcomes, etc.
- We usually do not do things that will not follow our reasons anyway, unless we are trying to be 'spontaneous'.
- Because strangers do things differently we seem to have a choice.
- The reasons we have are really to manage social outcomes and our social worlds.
- We do not weigh 'outcomes' and decide but follow pathways.
- So, reasons and beliefs always have a social ecology.

This is very common in everyday discourses, e.g. "He did it, so he must have had a reason for doing it!" or "You must have had a reason to do it!" This has therefore also been common in psychological explanations that have based themselves on common everyday discourses (V4.1).

Meaning

Finally (see also Chapter 5), we often 'experience' an 'inner self' related to our discourses about 'meaning' and 'meaningful'. And once again, the experiences are usually very real but the way we talk and think about and explain those experiences are not (they are Pathway 1). So, under what common life contexts do we call an experience 'meaningful' or attribute strong 'meaning' to something?

- When we cannot easily say what is happening or what we are doing, it can seem 'meaningful' or 'emotional'.
- If the experience fits with a story we have about our 'selves'.
- If the experience will impact on others in our context.
- If the experience fits our life 'value discourses' or 'emotional discourses'.
- If the experience makes a good story to tell others.
- If the experience comes with available justifications and reasons.
- If talking about the experience will make people listen and not challenge.
- If the experience is something that is not normal or boring.
- If the experience is something that only you are doing.
- If the experience links positively to your resource–social relationship pathways.

These are all real experiences and affect your life contexts and pathways, but the problem comes when they are talked about as having changed you 'inside'. What is meant is that they have changed the way you talk about you 'self' and 'identity', and they are meaningful therefore but in an external way.

And so ironically, to conclude, the best way to 'know thyself' (Temple of Delphi and Aristotle) is to know what external contexts, social and societal, have shaped how you act, talk, and think. This includes the difficult-to-observe cases of both being shaped by discourses and being shaped by societal structures.

References

I have included here those authors I have learned from to compile the material in this chapter (whether I agreed with them or not), but not explicitly cited herein.

Bamberg, M., de Fina, A., & Schiffrin, D. (2007). *Selves and identities in narrative and discourse*. Philadelphia, PA: John Benjamins.

Berger, H. M., & del Negro, G. P. (2004). *Identity and everyday life: Essays in the study of folklore, music, and popular culture*. Middletown, CO: Wesleyan University Press.

Bhatia, S., & Priya, K. R. (2018). Decolonizing culture: Euro-American psychology and the shaping of neoliberal selves in India. *Theory & Psychology, 28*, 645–668.

Bleuler E. (1911/1950). *Dementia praecox or the group of schizophrenias*. New York, NY: International Universities Press.

Descola, P. (2013). *The ecology of others*. Chicago, IL: Prickly Paradigm Press.

Geertz, C. (1966). *Person, time, and conduct in Bali: An essay in cultural analysis. Cultural Report Series No. 14*. Detroit, MI: Yale University.

Gergen, K. J. (1991). *The saturated self: Dilemmas of identity in contemporary life*. New York, NY: Basic Books.

Giddens, A. (1990). *The consequence of modernism*. Oxford: Polity Press.

Giddens, A. (1991). *Modernity and self-identity: Self and society in late modern age*. Oxford: Polity Press.

Glaskin, K. (2012). Anatomies of relatedness: Considering personhood in Aboriginal Australia. *American Anthropologist, 114*, 297–308.

Guerin, B. (2001). Individuals as social relationships: 18 ways that acting alone can be thought of as social behavior. *Review of General Psychology, 5*, 406–428.

Guerin, B. (2016). *How to rethink psychology: New metaphors for understanding people and their behavior*. London: Routledge.

Guerin, B., & Foster, T. M. (1994). Attitudes, beliefs and behavior: Saying you like, saying you believe, and doing. *Behavior Analyst, 17*, 127–129.

Heelas, P., & Lock, A. (Eds.) (1981). *Indigenous psychologies: The anthropology of self*. London: Academic Press.

Hodgkiss, P. (2011). *The making of the modern mind*. London: Athlone Press.

Holland, R. (1977). *Self & social context*. New York, NY: Macmillan.

Jackson, P., & Holbrook, B. (1995). Multiple meanings: Shopping and the cultural politics of identity. *Environment and Planning A, 27*, 1913–1930.

Lloyd, K. E. (1994). Do as I say, not as I do. *Behavior Analyst, 17*, 131–139.

Myers, F. R. (1991). *Pintupi country, Pintupi self: Sentiment, place, and politics among Western Desert Aborigines*. Los Angeles, CA: University of California Press.

Oakdale, S. (2005). *I foresee my life: The ritual performance of autobiography in an Amazonian community*. London: University of Nebraska Press.

Pickren, W. E. (2018). Psychology in the social imaginary of neoliberalism: Critique and beyond. *Theory & Psychology, 28*, 575–580.

Poirier, S. (2005). *A world of relationships: Itineraries, dreams, and events in the Australian Western Desert*. Toronto: University of Toronto Press.

Rose, N. (1996). *Inventing our selves: Psychology, power, and personhood*. Cambridge, UK: Cambridge University Press.

Scalabrini, A., Maucci, C., Esposito, R., Damiani, S., & Northoff, G, (2020). Dissociation as a disorder of integration: On the footsteps of Pierre Janet. *Progress in Neuropsychopharmacology & Biological Psychiatry, 101*, 1–12.

Siedentop, L. (2014). *Inventing the individual: The origins of Western liberalism*. London: Penguin Books.

Teo, T. (2018). *Homo neoliberalus*: From personality to forms of subjectivity. *Theory & Psychology, 28*, 581–599.

Verdouw, J. J. (2017). The subject who thinks economically? Comparative money subjectivities in neoliberal context. *Journal of Sociology, 53*, 523–540.

Walker, H. (2013). *Under a watchful eye: Self, power, and intimacy in Amazonia*. London: University of California Press.

6 A new look at Marxism, psychology, and social contextual analysis

This chapter discusses some relations between Marxism and social contextual analysis. Marx has been a major influence on all the social sciences but the few attempts to make the most important parts amenable to psychology have either not been overly convincing or else lacking in important explanations (Brown, 1974; Vygotsky, 1997). For example, Vygotsky repeated frequently that language use is social but was less convincing on the details of how exactly it was social, because, in fact, most language use looks like it is individualistic (but see V4.4). However, he also wrote that: "Psychology is in need of its own *Das Kapital*—its own concepts of class, basis, value etc.—in which it might express, describe, and study its object" (Vygotsky, 1997, p. 330)

In this chapter, I will focus on just a few major parts of Marx's work that I believe have not been discussed properly within psychology and look at them through social contextual analysis. The similarities are not accidental because many features of Marxist thought have already been part of pulling contextual analysis together in order to merge 'psychology' into the social sciences. But discussing this will also inform us as to why Marxist thought has not made progress in mainstream psychology, because there are major contradictions between the two. I will focus on four areas and then briefly go through a few others:

- How social contextual analysis has incorporated the importance of the means of production, the social relations of production, and the analysis of class.
- Dialectical materialism in contextual analysis.
- The role of ideology, consciousness, and language in Marxism, and how we can perhaps develop these in a new way.
- Class structures in context.

Social relations of production = resource–social relationship pathways

Those who have read Marx will know that the social relations of production are a major part of his work. Our economic systems have various means of production (family self-sustaining farms, factories, machinery) that 'we' need to produce our resources, and the point is that these in turn shape our social relationships. Family and community gardens led to all the kin-based behaviours common to social anthropological accounts of social behaviour. Industrialization and machinery led to the modernist world and stranger relationships that shape our current behaviours, while artificial intelligence (AI) and computers are shaping our behaviour in new ways for the future.

So how our resources are produced and distributed hugely shape human behaviour, but you will not find this in psychology texts (cf. Guerin, 2016a). We need to understand resources (means of production and distribution) and social relations together—this is one of Marx's main points in fact, that it is only idealism (language use) that allows human 'minds' to be considered separate from the material world. This basic shaping of our lives is included in social contextual analysis by emphasizing more than psychology ever has, how resources and the distribution of resources need to be studied through the different forms of social relationships, and vice versa. We are not individuals finding what we need and then also getting social relationships; we build resource–social relationship pathways because we can only get resources through our social relationships—they always go together, whether family or stranger relationships.

The ways in which different economies (resource production and distribution) are organized also produce different divisions of labour and at the same time this means divisions in social relationships. This is why *opportunity contexts* are so important to analyse in human social behaviour since many of our divisions into certain means of production (work, money, relationship opportunities) and social relations are already prefigured in our worlds even before we are born (as societal structures of opportunity, I do not mean as DNA, lol!).

All this is brought together by *focusing on exchanges of resources between people in social relationships* and tracking people's resource–social relationship pathways through their lives. This includes stranger relationships as well as family:

> The production of life, both of one's own in labour and of fresh life in procreation, now appears as a double relationship: on the one hand as a natural, on the other as a social relationship. By social we understand the co-operation of several individuals, no matter under what

conditions, in what manner and to what end. It follows from this that a certain mode of production, or industrial stage, is always combined with a certain mode of co-operation, or social stage, and this mode of co-operation is itself a "productive force". Further, that the multitude of productive forces accessible to men determines the nature of society, hence, that the "history of humanity" must always be studied and treated in relation to the history of industry and exchange.
(Marx & Engels, 1846, pp. 48–49)

That is, we must study social relationships within the contexts of economics, culture, etc. and, unlike psychology, include stranger social relationships not just familial:

economic base ←→ social relations
resources ←→ social relationships

This was put well by Gurvitch:

> From this point of view it is *entirely false to say that Marx reduced social life as a whole to economic life*. He did exactly the opposite. He revealed that economic life is only an integral part of social life, and that our conception of what takes place in economic life is falsified if we do not recognize that behind capital, the commodity, value, price, and the distribution of goods, society and the human beings who participate in it are concealed.
> (Gurvitch, 1983, pp. 40–41, italics in original)

Dialectical = contextual?

Another key part of Marxist thought comes with the terms 'dialectical materialism' and 'historical materialism'. There are many different interpretations of these, 'dialectics' in particular, and I will suggest one below that is a little different to others (Hegel, Lenin, Mao, etc.). For me, the gist of what is being argued with these terms in Marxist thought comprises different mixtures of these points:

- There are always many contexts leading to what humans do.
- Causal explanations in the social sciences do not work.
- Arguing with logic is not useful with contextual analyses because multiple things are always going on, and all the premises for the use of logic are contextual anyway.

- Searching for the *origins* of what humans do, does not explain what is happening now.
- Resources and social relationships are always involved together.
- What happens (history) is about material events, not thoughts, consciousness, or ideas existing independently of material events.
- There are always *opposing forces* acting on people, as well as strategies for these being played out (through resources and social relationships).
- Whatever you might find going on with human behaviour, there are always other forces to do things differently, or even do the opposite, being held in check or negotiated.
- Opposing forces are sometimes called 'contradictions' but they are not like logical contradictions, because they are about material events and what happens (history), not the abstractions of logic.

For example, if a government enforces certain rules in a punitive way, this immediately opens up strategies for resistance, which might be to oppose ('contradict') the rules or to find ways around the rules. This means that *the enforcement itself has produced its very contradiction* (as some Marxists would say), although it can also open up new resource–social relationship pathways for some people that are neither submission nor opposition. But the opposing forces and strategies are not 'contradictions' in a logical sense, as Marx emphasized, but real material happenings that are opposed. In fact, I will argue that there are no logical contradictions in the real world, they are fictions of discourse.

Conceptualizing contradictions and opposing forces in material action and real life

So, there are two ways 'contradiction' has been used, and I wish to suggest a third, which combines them based on the following: logical contradiction is a use of language and language has its material basis by getting people to do things through uses of resources—it does not get its material basis from the things it 'refers' to.

1. One use of 'contradiction' is 'in-the-world' contradiction (Marx, Lenin, and others) and is more like opposing or opposite forces that are acting on people. This is very materialist and grounded in real things, like a field (physics) or context idea really. Capitalism has created opposing forces on people and the environment. This can look like a contradiction, but is nothing like a logical contradiction. By raising the price of watermelons, I can provide an opposing (is contradictory really a good word here?) force on your wanting to eat watermelons.

2. The second form of contradiction is logical: *a therefore not (not a); there is either a watermelon or there is not a watermelon*. However, logic only works in a material sense in the following way: *if* you can get someone to agree with some premises first, then you can force them to agree with something else—a logical deduction. But logicians forget or trivialize the first part—how do I get someone to agree with my premises (see Chapter 1)? This makes logic useless for 'material proof' since it is all language-based, and you need to identify relations that are general ($a = a$) and therefore useless (ironically, Plekhanov, Deleuze, and Nietzsche all make these arguments). I will say more about this later, but the question really becomes: logic exists only in language, so *what is this form of language doing to people that has material (resource) outcomes*?

3. In *my* version, logical contradictions do not exist in the world. They are only materially real when we have real people who have been persuaded (a material social process) to agree on both opposing premises (e.g. you have to socially persuade them that there *is* a watermelon and that there is also *not* a watermelon). But this is all language and depends on the real material outcomes (power) of the social relationships involved in getting them persuaded in the first place. Otherwise logic is useless. But there cannot be both a watermelon and not a watermelon in the material world, that is just words or ideology. But in all this *there is still a real material conflict in the social relationship from the logic itself*. But the real material conflict going on is in *how someone was able to be persuaded of opposing premises*, and so there is (1) present anyway in (3)—opposing *social* forces (of persuasion) producing the logical contradiction (agreement on general premises).

So, there is really only one 'contradiction', the (1) of Marx, Lenin etc. (I think Mao confuses (1) and (2) in places). There are only opposing forces acting *materially in the world* and this can be analysed for both doing and talking. And by my (3), this subsumes logical contradiction when we stop thinking of it as existing outside of material social relations. To get *logical contradiction* in the first place requires material opposing (social) forces by which you can *persuade* someone to agree on both premises, but this is still a very material (social) process of negotiation. Only in this way can the use of logic have material effects on people and their social relationships, not otherwise.

So, what is wrong with logic?

Logic and dialectics are not in opposition, therefore, as Marx also said. Dialectics is not about being *illogical*, it is just saying that there are problems with the abstraction of logic that does not help in real life and material problems. Here are some of the problems, to summarize (see also V4.7):

- As Nietzsche (1967, section 512), Deleuze (1995), and Plekhanov (1929, p. 112) all wrote, logic is based upon using *premises*, *identity*, and *abstractions* and these have material effects on people only through discourse and hence they only have social relationship outcomes.
- In the real world we cannot assert any premises as true facts, since they are words or uses of language and just function to do things to people (they do not represent or substitute for the world), so the function of pure logic is already not useful; truth and falsity are not properties of words, just of doing things.
- Logic is therefore a *social practice*, based on a certain form of language use that *requires prior social persuasion of some premises*; as such, it is fairly useless in the real material world and is only useful in the social world of persuasion (you cannot use logic on your cat).
- Logic is further shown to be social/discursive and not materially useful because it relies on abstractions such as identity ($a = a$) and similar rules (*if a then b, therefore if not b then not a*); but in the material (non-discursive) world, such abstract formulations are either useless or nonsense, since the abstract and general 'a' is *not* always the same as itself (cat = cat is useless, because material cats are actually all different).

For Marx, however, as he repeatedly says, the premises in contextual or dialectical thinking are not language-based but must be observable material events (that is, not from persuasion), such as increasing the price of watermelons:

> The premises from which we begin are not arbitrary ones, not dogmas, but real premises from which abstraction can only be made in the imagination. They are the real individuals, their activity and the material conditions under which they live, both those which they find already existing and those produced by their activity. These premises can thus be verified in a purely empirical way.
> (Marx & Engels, 1846, pp. 36–37)

Completing Marx's removal of idealism and metaphysics

Most of the attempts to link Marxist thought to psychology have drawn on some of his earlier writings, mostly limited to the more philosophical Marx of *The German Ideology* and his early *Philosophical and Economic Manuscripts*. However, many people argue that Marx made a decisive split with discussing philosophy, 'consciousness', and similar notions after *The German Ideology* and did not write about such things again. Others argue that there was continuity and that Marx only stopped writing on these topics to concentrate on *Das Kapital*.

So why do these books seem especially relevant to psychology as currently defined? In *The German Ideology*, the *Economic and Philosophical Manuscripts*, the *Theses on Feuerbach*, and elsewhere, Marx sought to remove metaphysics, idealism, and ideology from his analyses and to make his analyses concrete, material, practical, and historical. In my terms, he was making a contextual analysis of the strands of Western philosophy of his day, including a discourse analysis of what was being said and written (cf. Guerin, 2016b). While this was successful in many ways, there are gaps between what he said at that time and later, and he was clearer on what was *wrong* with Western ways of thinking (correctly) than what was needed *to replace* it. This is the segment of his writings, I believe, that has led to disputes over whether he had a rupture or discontinuity in his thinking between the early Marx and the later Marx, or whether his thoughts were continuous (cf. Balibar, 2017, afterword).

The point of this is that it is these early passages that seem to make possible the construction of a 'Marxist psychology'. Some psychologists relish these books because they speak to seemingly 'internal' notions that still make up the fabric of past and current psychology (consciousness, awareness, etc.). This therefore appears to be a Pathway 1 Marx (V4.1) and he might join cognitive psychology in zipping along that Pathway 1 fork in the road! But if Marx dispensed with such notions as idealistic and fruitless, then this is basically saying that 'Marxist psychology' is a contradiction or oxymoron, and he was really following Pathway 2 all along (contextual or dialectical).

His basic argument was that all metaphysical terms are illusionary and should be replaced by descriptions of material social relations, especially the social relations involved in resource production. This, then, prefigured his extensive analyses just like this is suggested in *Das Kapital* and elsewhere, which focused on political economy (resources linked to societal/political social relationships). The main reason this looks like a rupture in his thinking is that many of the terms in his earlier works are hardly ever discussed again. This not only includes 'idealism' and 'metaphysics', but also terms like 'consciousness', 'thinking', and 'language', terms that later became embedded in the realm of Pathway 1 psychology. How Marx thought about these (based on his earlier works) is therefore pivotal in what a 'Marxist psychology' would look like (although I am arguing that this is an oxymoron since the whole idea of a 'psychology' separate from other social sciences is incompatible with Marxist thought and social contextual analysis). Some points to consider are as follows:

1. One view of the 'rupture' is that he had *solved* the issues of these terms in his early writings and did not need to address them again.
2. A second view is that he became preoccupied with the more important task of analysing the social and economic conditions of capitalism and did not follow these ideas through any further.
3. A third idea is that there were complexities when trying to shift from Pathway 1 (ideology) to Pathway 2, which Marx *did not know how to fix*, and so he wisely moved on rather than wasting time arguing further with philosophy and the abstractions. However, these complexities have not been solved by anyone in psychology, so they remain points of contention.

So, I wish to suggest some ways we can resolve these and move on, like Marx did with economics, to the more detailed social, economic, and cultural analyses of human life, rather than stay stuck in an ideology of human 'psychology' (Pathway 1). To do this *we need to show more concretely that language, thought and 'consciousness' are material events* and not abstractions, ideologies, or promises of future brain events (which is what V4 was all about). Doing this I think would satisfy Marx's early writings as well as his later works.

My particular concern is that I believe (3), *Marx did not have a solution as to how 'consciousness' or 'thinking' were actually material social relationships*. These appear somewhat awkwardly both in his later works (rarely) and even in the early Marxist writings (see the following two examples), since consciousness and thinking appear in most Western philosophy and even current psychology as inherently idealist and essentialist concepts that do not have an observable material basis (Pathway 1). Just *repeating* that 'they are based in real social relations', as both Marx and Vygotsky did, is correct but does not help much without details, especially when overwhelmed by psychologies that are still based on unobservable, hypothetical 'inner' events (like Vygotsky's 'inner speech'). The following applies a way of thinking about 'thinking' and 'consciousness' to make it observable and material (V4 has much more).

The following are some examples where it is not clear what Marx means:

> Mr Proudhon understands perfectly well that men manufacture worsted, linens and silks; and whatever credit is due for understanding such a trifle! What Mr Proudhon does not understand is that, according

to their faculties, men also *produce the social relations* in which they produce worsted and linens. Still less does Mr Proudhon understand that those who produce social relations in conformity with their material productivity also produce the *ideas, categories, i.e. the ideal abstract expressions of those same social relations*. Indeed, the categories are no more eternal than the relations they express. They are historical and transitory *products*. To Mr Proudhon, on the contrary, the prime cause consists in abstractions and categories. According to him it is these and not men which make history. *The abstraction, the category regarded as such*, i.e. as distinct from man and his material activity, is, of course, immortal, immutable, impassive. It is nothing but an entity of pure reason, which is only another way of saying that an abstraction, regarded as such, is abstract. An admirable *tautology!*

(Marx, 1975, p. 95, my italics)

The production of ideas, of conceptions, of consciousness, is at first *directly interwoven* with the material activity and the material intercourse of men, the language of real life. Conceiving, thinking, the mental intercourse of men, appear at this stage as *the direct efflux of their material behaviour*. The same applies to mental production as expressed in the language of politics, laws, morality, religion, metaphysics, etc., of a people. Men are *the producers of their conceptions, ideas*, etc.—real, active men, as they *are conditioned by a definite development of their productive forces* and of the intercourse corresponding to these, up to its furthest forms. Consciousness *can never be* anything else than *conscious existence*, and the existence of men is their actual life-process. ...

We set out from real, active men, and on the basis of their real life-process we demonstrate the development of the *ideological reflexes and echoes* of this life-process. The *phantoms formed in the human brain* are also, necessarily, *sublimates of their material life-process*, which is empirically verifiable and *bound to* material premises. Morality, religion, metaphysics, all the rest of ideology and their *corresponding forms of consciousness*, thus no longer retain the semblance of independence. They have no history, no development; but men, developing their material production and their material intercourse, *alter, along with this their real existence, their thinking* and the products of their thinking. Life is not determined by consciousness, but consciousness by life.

(Marx & Engels, 1846, p. 42, my italics)

So, while I do not disagree with the gist of these passages trying to link thinking and consciousness to a material basis, the parts in italic show how vague and hedging this all is ("the mental intercourse of men, appear at this stage as the direct efflux of their material behaviour"!). We can do much better, and the social contextual approach to thinking provides, I believe, a much better *material basis for language use and therefore thinking and consciousness* as well, based on real material outcomes from other people and discursive communities. I will walk you through some of these points in what follows, which were developed and elaborated further in V4.4. The aim is to describe more concretely how 'thinking', 'consciousness', etc., are real material events and not ideology.

Individual humans have material relationships with inanimate objects and also with other people, through the *consequences* or *outcomes* of those events changing the context in some way. We can open doors for ourselves to get through and we can open the door for an elderly person; the two actions look the same but functionally they are different because the events change the world in different ways as material consequences (one gets us outside, the other helps our relationship in many ways with both the elderly person and the others watching). This is material, and the material effects or consequences of our actions then guide, shape, or channel our future actions.

Humans also learn language, and, in fact, *overlearn* language, but this is simply another special case of having relationships with other people through outcomes or consequences changing the world (which we learn through years of learning). Cats do not teach us the word 'cat', people do. The responses or outcomes we get to the word 'cat' can only be material effects or changes arising *from what other people do* who have learned the language behaviours in the same way. Our saying 'cat' gets no material effects or consequences from a cat; but it can get material consequences from other people who speak our language.

In this way, *our uses of language are material (social) events* because they have real, material *social* consequences or *social* effects—but they only get these from another person who has learned that language also and they can be unrelated to what is said. If we have those conditions, and some ongoing material reciprocity in the social relationship, then language use is merely another way of doing things in this world that has material consequences that alter the world a bit. *Language is a socially transitive verb*, not an abstract noun.

We hugely overlearn our uses of language so that whatever events happens in our lives, some talking (or thinking) is usually the first and foremost response we have, and we usually have multiple different verbal responses simultaneously because we have learned to respond for different audiences. That is, the first thing we now do in life is *talk* about what is happening.

These are social responses, remember, so they only relate to the material social situations we are experiencing in life. With contradictory social relationships we can be shaped to have contradictory ways of talking and thinking. But they are really *conflicting* or *opposing* responses and not actually logical (or even 'cognitive') contradictions (as we saw earlier), since in front of the different audiences separately we can say one of those contradictory things and there is no conflict. They are only *conflicting* if both audiences are present simultaneously (or both situations or life events): they produce opposing consequences from each audience that we need to analyse contextually (dialectically).

Moving now to *thinking*. Moreover, I can open a door for someone *even when no one is going out* or I do not want to go out. As mentioned, this is different from opening a door for yourself to get through, but we learn the response so well we can do it when no one else is there. It does require a special context for it to occur, however: "Show me how you get the door open for Mrs Jones so her walker can fit through".

So, in the same way, I can have the conversations and talking I normally have with other people *even when they are not there*, and we can even hear them talk when they are not there. This is a key point, and a difficult one. Difficult because *this is what constitutes thinking and consciousness* and doing these conversations without anyone there *is still a material, social relation;* it has not become something inner, idealistic, internal, or metaphysical (V4.4).

But through Western history at least, such conversing when no one is there has been wrongly considered *non-material* and *metaphysically different* to talking in front of someone. However, we would never argue that opening a door as if for an elderly person when no one is actually there is non-material or metaphysical; we only argue this when conversing when no one is there. Such material events have usually been conveniently placed 'in the head or mind', although this make no real sense. But *thinking is just talking without saying things out loud*, and this is materially the same as talking out loud (except no one does anything *immediately,* but it can have a direct effect by avoiding people doing something by not saying out loud; see Box 4.2 in V4.4).

And this is the false bases of idealisms, the *cogito*, cognitive processing models more recently, and all the older mind, soul, and psyche notions. It is also the material basis in social relationships for what is called consciousness. When we are 'doing' thinking or consciousness, we are 'doing' conversations but without the other people being present, and this is not taking place 'inside' us *but arises from our history of social relations in a material way*, since these social relations have shaped these absent conversations by their consequences, not by some 'inner determinant'. They have been shaped and overlearned through material consequences from our social relationships.

Thinking and consciousness are therefore *concrete, in the world,* and *social,* as they are having material conversations but with no one there—they are not metaphysical, inside our heads, and non-social. They are also potentially observable, since I just need to observe your current external contexts very, very carefully to know what conversations you are likely to be having—whether or not anyone is there (Guerin, 2016b). In practice this would be difficult, but the point is that if I were to know your detailed material contexts, I would know what you are thinking.

With this view, we can see better how talking and thinking are purely social, and this includes all types of talking and thinking, including what are called consciousness, ideology, beliefs, cognition, etc. So, talking and thinking have a real material basis, albeit exclusively with social outcomes, which is in the consequences of our social relations, just as Marx saw. The training and over-shaping of language use between peoples over many years of our lives is the concrete material basis for this, not a mind or consciousness acting as an independent or metaphysical agent or subject.

I have argued, as Marx suggested but without giving details, that there is indeed a material basis for our thinking and 'consciousness' and it is *in our social relations,* but he was vague as to how to work this through. When someone reports thinking or talking, we must observe and analyse where this language use has been shaped, what audiences or discursive communities were involved, and what this language use is doing in their world (the outcomes or the consequences that in turn alter the world in some way). This is why I think Marx knew *what* he was trying to say (consciousness and thinking have an external social material basis) but not *how* to justify that or to convince people. He was stuck between Pathway 1 and Pathway 2.

So, language is a socially transitive verb. We need to think of and research *language as doing something that has material social outcomes that alter the world.* For example, the parts taught as grammar and syntax are about how we can allow language to work better and quicker (like how easy it is to open a door, or does it get stuck regularly), and pragmatics and discourse analysis are about *what we do with language once we have spent many years learning*—what do we do to people with our uses of language? How do we utilize language to get people to do things for resource production or distribution, or for developing social relations?

All the different 'forms' of language exist because they are doing slightly different things to people (poetry, prose, conversation, suggestions, song, argument, therapy talk, hypnosis, shaman ritual, science talk and writing, drama, reminiscing, advertising, political oratory, magic spells). All this means is that they have different social consequences that alter the world so we behave differently in future.

We can now go back to the beginning and link language use, thinking, consciousness, ideology, and 'mind' to Marx's main task of analysing social relations and resource production together—the resource–social relationship pathways of life. The system of language is learned so we can get people who speak that language to do things or to control them to reduce their opportunities (class structuring). This, I believe, fills the links Marx could never articulate about the social-material basis for language, thinking, consciousness, beliefs, categories, and ideas. The material basis is not our brain, but in the material outcomes of our social relationships.

Class structures in context

> The concentration of attention upon cultural analysis and ideology-critique in much recent Marxist theory has itself attracted criticism from those who see in this orientation a distorted view of the ways in which class domination is maintained, in so far as this is explained by the effects of a dominant ideology rather than by economic control and political power.
>
> (Bottomore & Goode, 1983, p. 162)

Another major feature of Marx's thought was about the fundamental problem of capitalism creating class divisions in society that then get perpetuated to the advantage of a few. If we are to produce a new or merged 'psychology' (move to Pathway 2), then this fundamental insight needs to be included: that *people are shaped into groups of behaviours and life patterns not of their own making but by societal structures.*

This is extremely difficult to do within current forms of psychology, since people's thought and actions are said to originate inside their private and individual self, so in principle they can always 'decide' to 'opt out' of such shaping. Once we include the shaping contexts of opportunities, and especially the societally and economically imposed opportunities, we have class, race, gender, and other structures available for analysis and change (Chapter 3).

Further, with language viewed as a material social practice, we can also analyse (social analysis, language analysis, and discourse analysis; SALADA) the way discourse communities shape us to use class and other distinctions so freely (V4.3). That is, the language practices around class and other categories (ideologies) are materially based in social practices and privilege.

Summary

The point of this chapter is not to say that Marxism and social contextual analysis are the same, they are not. Marx spent most of his time analysing political economies and how they worked. While frequently remarking on how this affects individuals and usually makes their lives worse, that was not his focus, at least not after the earlier phase.

What is important is that Marx created some of the fundamental points of any social science analyses and attempts to write a 'Marxist psychology' have not worked because there are fundamental contradictions (material and logical) between the two. This was a clear objective when synthesizing the social contextual analyses to use and integrate Marx's main points.

There are many other integrative points and mere similarities that could be discussed but will be left to others to develop: alienation and language (see V6), how we can only learn through practical activities with the world and with people, and the relations between 'individuals' and society (see Chapter 2).

References

I have included here those authors I have learned from to compile the material in this chapter (whether I agreed with them or not), but not explicitly cited herein.

Althusser, L. (2007). *On ideology*. London: Verso.
Balibar, E. (2017). *The philosophy of Marx*. London: Verso.
Bottomore, T., & Goode, P. (Eds.) (1983). *Readings in Marxist sociology*. Oxford: Clarendon Press.
Brown, P. (1974). *Towards a Marxist psychology*. New York, NY: Harper Colophon Books.
Coward, R., & Ellis, J. (1977). *Language and materialism: Developments in semiology and the theory of the subject*. London: Routledge & Kegan Paul.
Deleuze, G. (1968). *Difference and repetition*. New York, NY: Columbia University Press.
Deleuze, G. (1995). *Negotiations, 1972–1990*. New York, NY: Columbia University Press.
Godlier, M. (2011). *The mental and the material: Thought, economy and society*. London: Verso.
Guerin, B. (2016a). *How to rethink human behavior: A practical guide to social contextual analysis*. London: Routledge.
Guerin, B. (2016b). *How to rethink psychology: New metaphors for understanding people and their behavior*. London: Routledge.
Gurvitch, G. (1983). Marx's sociology. In T. Bottomore & P. Goode (Eds.), *Readings in Marxist sociology* (pp. 38–43). Oxford: Clarendon Press.

Hekman, S. (2010). *The material of knowledge: Feminist disclosures.* Bloomington, IN: Indiana University Press.

Marx, K. (1975). Letter from Marx to Pavel Vasilyevich Annenkov. In K. Marx & F. Engels, *Marx and Engels Collected Works* (Vol. 38, pp. 95–98). Moscow: International Publishers.

Marx, K., & Engels, F. (1846). *The German ideology.*

Nietzsche, F. (1967). *The will to power.* London: Penguin.

Plekhanov, G. (1929). *Fundamental problems of Marxism.* New York, NY: International Publishers.

Silverman, D., & Torode, B. (1980). *The material word: Some theories of language and its limits.* London: Routledge & Kegan Paul.

Vološinov, V. N. (1973). *Marxism and the philosophy of language.* London: Harvard University Press.

Vygotsky, L. (1997). The historical meaning of the crisis in psychology. In R. W. Rieber & J. Wollock (Eds.), *The collected works of L. S. Vygotsky: Problems of the theory and history of psychology* (pp. 233–343). New York, NY: Plenum Press.

7 Contextualizing the arts

In this book I am trying to show how human actions, talking, and thinking, which have been treated by psychology as internal to humans and mostly originating in the brain, are really shaped externally by resources coming through social and societal relationships. Moreover, I am attempting to highlight that if we utilize what the social sciences have learned over a hundred and more years, we can fill out more concrete accounts than the individualistic versions propagated by psychology that use abstract language as a hedge.

We have already seen that most of the more complicated analyses, which typically get left to such abstract 'internal' theorizing, have their material base in human social relationships and what these do for our resources. For example, we have seen that beliefs are not something we 'decide' and then 'possess' inside us but are discourses we say and think that have been shaped and reshaped externally by the people and media around us—we do things to people using our beliefs; we can do all our social behaviours *using* beliefs. And we saw the same for 'self', that it is not some 'thing' inside us that we learn or reveal or discover inside. Rather, it is also just a way we talk and think that does things to people—most noticeably to negotiate our social relationships for resources.

Most of the human activities that make little sense, and hence are placed solely in abstract 'inner' worlds in order to 'explain' them, are really about dealing with social, cultural, discursive, and societal relationships, since these are difficult to observe directly. Just as for beliefs and the 'self', so it is for *the arts* and *religion*—two of the most common human behaviours but that are difficult to 'explain'—even to explain why humans would do them at all. In the same way that people hang on to their beliefs and their sense of self regardless of rationality, but this then turns out to be because of *social* shaping (see Chapter 1), so it is that people also spend a lot of their time and money on music, paintings, fiction, and the many religious behaviours, which some would argue seem to do very little and it is difficult to explain why people do them.

Just as for language and thinking (V4.4; see also Chapter 7), most analyses of art look for a material base that originates the behaviours but can only find the written words in the case of language, and the 'art objects' or musical sounds in the case of the arts. Instead, then, the material base is put inside the person, usually into the brain as the originator or a 'pleasure' centre supposedly driving these activities. But as we saw for the previous examples, there are really two types of material base involved here in originating the behaviours:

- The object itself.
- What *people* do when they see or hear art, how that changes social relationships, and ongoing reciprocities (remembering that this now includes the all-important stranger relationships).

For all of these, like language, most everyday and academic 'explanations' focus on the first since it is easier and quicker to observe, and then make abstract models and fictions to bypass the second. This means looking for 'structural' patterns (see Chapter 2) in the topographies of art objects that are then turned tautologically into explanations.

So, art activities are mostly like language—they only function to change people but it is difficult to see where the 'power' for this to happen comes from. For language, people often think that the words themselves make people do things, or that our thinking makes *us* do things, but we saw elsewhere why these two ideas are false (V4.3, V4.4; see also Chapter 5).

We will find in what follows that the same wrong attributions occur for the arts (and religious behaviours) as well—that art moves us because of something about the physical paintings or sounds, and that performing religious rituals or the religious symbols are themselves the source of power to change people. And once again, then, like language, we will find that the real power to do things to people with the arts and religious behaviours comes from the multiple ongoing links between social relationships and resources, and the reciprocities that keep us in functioning social relationships for other outcomes.

This question of the material base that shapes the behaviours of the arts is a perennial one in the philosophy of art (Collingwood, 1938; Guerin, 2019; Morphy, 2007; Orwell, 2008; Plekhanov, 1953; Vygotsky, 1974). In general, the answer is the same as for language and thinking (Guerin, 2016, V4.3, V4.4): the origin and shaping of art behaviours arises from their material use in negotiating social relationships and resources, not from the objects or sounds themselves. That is where their 'power' to do things to people and to change people comes from.

Contextualizing the arts

Even though I argue that there are no hidden powers within the physical artworks themselves, or within the musical sounds themselves, this does not mean that art is not powerful. Art can be very powerful to make people do things, it is just that the power does not come from the art objects or sounds themselves (Orwell, 2008). The power or 'value creating' (Morphy, 2007) of art arises from the social relationships involved and the ongoing social reciprocities and outcomes of these. This is how art can do things to people. But what is most interesting is that the art and musical forms can do things to people that using language cannot (V4.7)!

So, like language (V4.3), *the arts only do things to people*; that is, we must analyse how these activities fit into the resource–social relationship pathways in our lives. There is no direct effect from the world itself when we make musical sounds or put paint on paper (Guerin, 2019). An eggplant does not grow quicker if I play it a C major arpeggio. Cats do not respond differentially if we put a Picasso in front of them. You cannot make coffee just by doing a painting. We only do things to *people* with art; that is our starting point.

This means that there will be no *clear* division between how we do things to people with art or with any other ways, but we call some ways of affecting people 'art' under certain conditions. For example, whatever the effects of art, these change over time and the same art does not do the same things to every person nor even the same things at different times to the same person.

This already contrasts strongly with language (V4.3). Regular language (excluding poetry, for example) is a specialized way of getting (or trying to get) people to do:

- very *precise* actions, talking, and thinking;
- which can be replicated across large groups of people in standard ways;
- with pictures and sounds that are tightly controlled (26 English letters);
- and with intense training of grammar (see Chapter 1) so this can all be done very quickly and with fewer errors.

There is no point having a language such that saying "Please make me some coffee" will one day lead to the listener getting you coffee but another day the same listener will get you some popcorn. Or more accurately, we would no longer call it a language if it had those properties. But this is how art is!

So, an initial problem is: why would people bother spending so much time, money, and effort in their lives producing art behaviours that have vague, ever-changing, and often unknown effects on other people?

> If I could express the same thing with words as with music, I would, of course, use a verbal expression. Music is something autonomous and much richer. Music begins where the possibilities of language end. That is why I write music.
>
> (Sibelius, 1919)

The differences between art and language, and between the different forms of what we call art, therefore lie in what you do differently to people and the outcomes that function to maintain those behaviours, talking, or thinking. But we know already that these outcomes are not certain, precise, or singular.

From the contextual analyses so far in this volume (see also V4.5–7), some main functions of art would be variations on these (as starting points only):

- distraction, escape, avoidance, or entertainment from other behaviours;
- shaping people to do/see things in new ways, which might help them;
- to use when words fail or do not work;
- providing discourses based around the artwork to assist in negotiating *unrelated* resource–social relationship pathways (Bourdieu, 1984).

The first and the last point in this list are common to a number of human behaviours, but the second and third are more unique to the arts. The visual and graphic arts, in particular, are able to reshape our very perceptual responses and shape us to look differently within our worlds (V4.5). With a contextual view, perception is always just a part of doing anything at all, so changing how and when we focus and look will change many or all our other behaviours, since perception is always involved—it is not a separate event (V4.5).

When we repeatedly study Picasso's paintings, for example, our eyes and all the perceptual responses can be reshaped to focus and telescope (V4.5) in *new* ways that our ordinary vistas do not shape us to do. We can then even see *familiar* objects in new ways because our very ways of looking have new response patterns. Picasso's paintings are not primarily to reshape or retrain how we *talk*, but to reshape our very perceptual responding (although observing people in art galleries would suggest the opposite). Poetry, on the other hand, can have many effects, but one is to reshape how we listen to, read, and use our 'normal' language (Guerin, 2020).

Contextualizing the arts 123

On the third function above, as I have stressed elsewhere (V4.3, V4.7; see also Chapter 1), our current world relies heavily on our use of language and the grammar that makes getting people to do things this way both quick and accurate. But using language for almost everything also provides many problems and challenges (V4.7), for example:

- There are 'gaps' in the world that language cannot 'say' at all.
- There are events and experiences that language cannot 'say'.
- There are sometimes social punishing effects of using language that prevent us from being able to do things to people in this way.
- The world changes and our language cannot cover or keep up with these changes easily, even though we keep twisting 'proper' language to have new effects on people, which current language cannot do (and is a major function of poetry; Guerin, 2020).
- When social relationships and their reciprocities (of all sorts) are failing, then the 'power' of words to do things to people also fails (V6.4, V6.6).

Unfortunately, in order to get people to do things when words fail in any of these ways, bullying and violent means are often used instead; we 'push' people to get things done because we cannot use words. But *the arts have always been there as alternative ways of affecting people without 'normal' uses of language* (treating poetry and theatre here as non-normal uses of language), although usually both are used in tandem.

Finally, the fourth option above, 'doing' art creates life situations that provide discourses and contexts that can be used to help form and maintain most of our social behaviours (Bourdieu, 1984; Rowe, 2018; Rowe & Guerin, 2018). That is, we can 'do' most of our social behaviours utilizing the arts. This is seen in visitors to art galleries 'seeing' a painting, naming what is 'represented' in the painting, and moving on. This is also echoed in the words of John Blacking, as we saw in Chapter 4: "A musical system should first be analysed not in comparison with other musics, but rather in relation to other social and symbolic systems within the same society" (Blacking, 1995, p. 228). The following list gives some exploratory examples of how we can do our main social behaviours utilizing the arts. There is a lot more to be explored.

- *Competing*: since the arts do not have precise or consistent effects on people it is easy to set up verbal competitions around both the appreciation of and knowledge of the arts. The arts can therefore provide a platform for playing our competitions for resources and social relationships.

- *Cooperating*: sharing similar 'tastes' in the arts can be utilized to help cooperating in other parts of life. This is especially prevalent in sharing music during cooperative tasks.
- *Bonding*: like 'collaborative talk', sharing art 'tastes' is a good form of bonding when beginning social relationships and when trying to manage ongoing social relationships. This can make up superficial or usurping strategies, as well as sincere ones. Again, sharing similar music is a common form.
- *Bullying*: competition over forms of art can develop into forms of bullying, in which 'superior' forms of art can be utilized. "Your music sucks!"
- *Image management*: the arts have a unique and common place in shaping self-presentations to develop and maintain resource–social relationship pathways. As well as negotiating via beliefs (see Chapter 5), the use of the arts is easy to hedge and be flexible.
- *Sharing*: sharing common 'tastes' in music, novels, poetry, or painting can be used to give something to each other for people in social relationships. This also includes sharing stories, beliefs, and opinions about the arts.
- *Agreeing*: relationships can be maintained or strengthened by agreeing and talking about how the arts are prevalent and important.
- *Distancing*: you can use the arts to break relationships or distance yourself by doing the above in reverse.
- *Reciprocating*: the arts are often used as gifts in giving paintings and music to each other (more than just sharing). You can also, in a sense, reciprocate by giving someone a new 'genre': "I give you this book of Klee's drawings that I think you will like"; "You should listen to some of the earlier Pink Floyd CDs, I think you'll like them as much as I do" (this last includes a bit of bonding by sharing as well).
- *Hedging*: lessening the impact of doing things to people can be done by having music playing or by putting the requests into poetic or music forms.
- *Protecting*: "Stay away from any modern classical music after the 1910s! It will only hurt your ears!"; "Look, go home and listen to your metal music, it will make you feel better."
- *Complaining*: with the arts you can sit around for long hours discussing music, poetry, or painting, and complaining about all the bad and superficial art (since you know better!).
- *Controlling*: given the arbitrariness or flexibility or the arts, doing the arts and discourses around art can be used to control people around you. Whereas some beliefs (see Chapter 4) can be challenged with evidence (though this is unlikely to succeed without the right social

reciprocities), the arts are more open. People can control those around them if they can use their resources to become the 'mover and shaker' in terms of arts.

- *Conflicting*: doing arts, or having discourses around the arts, can also be utilized to exacerbate or start conflicts. It should be obvious (often not to the protagonists) that such disputes are about other resource–social relationship conflicts.
- *Being polite*: adopting other people's preferences in the arts, at least in the short term, can be a way showing politeness. "No, you can choose the music to play tonight."
- *Being rude*: conversely, it is easy to be rude to someone through the arts, especially in discourses around the arts.
- *Being humorous*: because of the arbitrariness or flexibility of the arts, it is easy to base humour on, including parodies of musical patterns.
- *Inducing positive and negative emotions*: while our performances of emotions around music and other arts are largely arbitrary (Guerin, 2019), once established in a discursive community they can be utilized to 'induce' emotions. So musical sounds are not inherently sad or happy but within a community they can act that way.
- *Showing off*: in the arts, showing off can occur through both the performances and the discourses (Bourdieu, 1984; Kingsbury, 1988). This can then be utilized for social relationships and resources beyond the original context.
- *Humbling*: the arts can be used to make yourself look humble, especially because of their ambiguity. "I really do not know much about painting, certainly not as much as you do".

References

Blacking, J. (1995). *Music, culture, & experience: Selected papers of John Blacking.* Chicago, IL: University of Chicago Press.

Bourdieu, P. (1984). *Distinction: A social critique of the judgement of taste.* London: Routledge.

Collingwood, R. G. (1938). *The principles of art.* London: Oxford University Press.

Guerin, B. (2016). *How to rethink human behavior: A practical guide to social contextual analysis.* London: Routledge.

Guerin, B. (2019). Contextualizing music to enhance music therapy. *Revista Perspectivas em Análise Comportamento, 10,* 222–242.

Guerin, B. (2020). What does poetry do to readers and listeners, and how does it do this? Language use as social activity and its clinical relevance. *Revista Brasileira de Análise do Comportamento, 15.*

Kingsbury, H. (1988). *Music, talent, and performance: A conservatory cultural system.* Philadelphia, PA: Temple University Press.

Morphy, H. (2007). *Becoming art: Exploring cross-cultural categories*. New York, NY: Berg.
Orwell, G. (2008). *All art is propaganda*. New York, NY: Harcourt.
Plekhanov, G. V. (1953). *Art and social life*. New York, NY: Lawrence & Wishart.
Rowe, P. (2018). *Heavy metal youth identities: Researching the musical empowerment of youth transitions and psychosocial wellbeing*. London: Emerald.
Rowe, P., & Guerin, B. (2018). Contextualizing the mental health of metal youth: A community for social protection, identity and musical empowerment. *Journal of Community Psychology*, *46*, 1–13.
Sibelius, J. (1919, 10 June). Interview with *Berlingske Tidende*. Retrieved from www.sibelius.fi/suomi/index.html.
Vygotsky, L. S. (1974). *The psychology of art*. New York, NY: MIT Press.

8 Contextualizing religion and religious behaviours

Religion is either universal or extremely widespread, and religious people claim that it is one of the most important activities in their life. Depending upon the particular variety of religion, religious activities can take up much time, money, and effort in human life. For these reasons alone, religion is a key human activity to analyse.

Religion and religious behaviours are also another topic that is studied perfectly well in the contextual social sciences, but of which Pathway 1 psychologies, I argue, have made a mess. As seen in V4.1, the Pathway 1 responses by psychology to the Gestalt problems were as follows:

1. Go back again to *studying what the brain does* since the brain must be where these more complex organizational units are constructed and so the answers will lie there.
2. Since we cannot see what is going on in the brain, then do what the computer scientists were doing at that time, and *build simulations, models, and theories of what might be going on internally* and try and test these with whatever observable responses can be measured.
3. Just *use the everyday or common language of the bigger units* even if we do not know anything about their reality; talk using the same words as ordinary people do and do not bother to analyse further. Understand what people do purely in terms of how they talk about it, and take what people say about 'human psychology' as descriptions of what it is we must study, our 'subject matter' is based on everyday conceptions.

The discussions of religion and religious behaviours in psychology have mostly been in terms of (3), but with some models following (2). Some, like William James (1902/1958), even used the neurology of his day to suggest brain bases to religion and religious behaviours. More recently the inevitable happened, and we now have response (1):

> The neuroscience of religion, also known as neurotheology and as spiritual neuroscience, attempts to explain religious experience and behaviour in neuroscientific terms. It is the study of correlations of neural phenomena with subjective experiences of spirituality and hypotheses to explain these phenomena.
>
> (Wikipedia, n.d.)

As usual, this is only correlational and promises of what *might* be found out one day. I look forward to better things from a neuroscience that follows Pathway 2.

The psychological study of religion and religious behaviours are good examples of psychology following Pathway 1. All the same errors occur, and we find again that social anthropology and sociology have been ahead for decades in contextualizing religion and religious behaviours. They are a good example of how to move current psychology from Pathway 1 to Pathway 2, and why it must be merged into the social sciences.

Here are the main points for doing this:

- Observe the actual behaviours seen or heard, and not just what people report are the behaviours.
- Spend time observing and participating if possible.
- Contextualize the actions, talking, and thinking over *all* contexts, including the societal ones (see Chapter 3).
- Where there are 'irrational' looking behaviours, treat these as having hidden social contexts (V1.7; see also Chapters 1 and 5).
- Listen to what people say about religion and religious behaviours but analyse them as discourses not as accurate descriptions or reports (SALADA; see V1.3).
- Analyse the societal shaping of any behaviours even though these might be hidden and not immediately obvious (see Chapter 3); looking for stratifications and restrictions can help this search.
- When there is a static-looking structure found, look for the flexible functioning (see Chapter 2), how it might change over time or context (in this case, religious and church structures are examples: "The Catholic church has a fixed structure"; Wallis, 1975a, p. 30).
- Be careful of attributing any functionality to the behaviours since there might be several, they might have changed, and they might be hidden without easy contextual observations.

The behaviours observed

There are many behaviours that have variously been called religious: church membership, church attendance, rituals, taboos, totem behaviours, praying, devotion, spiritual experiences, magic, and reading scriptures. While some sociologists and anthropologists have tried to distinguish among these different behaviours, I will include them all because, as will become clear, I do not wish to discriminate between religious and non-religious behaviours, let alone any of these finer categories.

Definitions of religion are very broad. Consider one definition of religion:

> Religion is a human phenomenon that unites cultural, social, and personality systems into a meaningful whole. Its components generally include (1) *a community of believers* who share (2) a common *myth* that interprets the abstractions of cultural values into historic reality through (3) *ritual behavior*, which makes possible personal participation in (4) a dimension of experience recognized as encompassing something more than everyday reality—*the holy*. These elements are united into recognizable *structures* that undergo *processes* of change, development, and deterioration.
>
> (Hargrove, 1989, pp. 29–30, italics in original)

Religion has many component behaviours that are difficult to distinguish conceptually, and no single feature defines religion. Sociologists and anthropologists (Malinowski, 1925/1948) have at times tried to distinguish between religion and magic, but others blur this distinction also (Homans, 1941; Nadel, 1957).

Some functions of religious behaviours

Pathway 1: the 'internal' functions of religious behaviours

When we look at the structures and functions claimed for religion, we again see current psychology focusing on functions originating *inside* people: 'being' religious or 'doing religious behaviours' have internal effects on individuals and these supposedly control and maintain the behaviours. "My faith is important to me, that is why I am religious." Not necessarily wrong, but this does not explain anything. In line with this, Child and Child (1993) listed the major functions in the literature as follows: therapeutic value for personal, interpersonal, and disease problems; increases in power, prestige, and admiration; confidence and greater chance of success; food taboos for helping child birth; initiation rituals that model acceptance of mature behaviours; grief processes in mortuary rituals to help recovery; and conformity with food sharing to help in starvation conditions. All Pathway 1 and internal.

Freud (1934) included many of the same functions but emphasized a very commonly made argument that people are insecure and anxious about the universe and life, and that religion reduces their anxiety so that they are "feeling comfortable morally" (Riches, 1994, p. 386). This Pathway 1 theme of religious behaviours functioning to reduce individual anxiety or uncertainty about the world is probably the most common theme in discussions about the functions of religion. It is also perhaps the most unexamined theme. Hamilton presents a typical presentation:

> The need to understand stems from emotional sources and may in certain circumstances reach a high degree of intensity. Not to understand is to be bewildered, confused and threatened. The human psyche is such that uncertainty, feelings of unfamiliarity and a sense of the alien are deeply disquieting and discomforting. We do not just seek to understand our world and our place in it out of mere interest; we need to know who and what we are and what place we occupy within the world. Religions seek answers to existential questions which go to the heart of our sense of identity, worth and purpose.
>
> (Hamilton, 1995, pp. 216–217)

What I wish to do next is to provide some better contexts: that religious behaviours are primarily social behaviours shaped by groups or communities; that religion is not, in principle, different to non-religious behaviour; and that the major theories that have been put forward to explain religious behaviours can be reversed so that social context (Pathway 2) can better be seen as the determinants rather than an inner religious determination (Pathway 1). In particular, I want to present an alternative interpretation of religious functioning to the one that is so common—that of escape from anxiety and uncertainty (Pathway 1), which also underlies cognitive psychology (Guerin, 2001, V4.8).

So what we will find is that the major function is really about holding a group together (kin-based originally but now the more difficult stranger-based), and that this is vital for all resource–social relationship pathways in life so the behaviours are important—even the non-religious equivalents we will see.

Pathway 2: the social functions of religion

There are many arguments and much evidence for the social basis of religion (Firth, 1996; Radcliffe-Brown, 1952; Tawney, 1938). First, there is historical evidence that religions originally had a primary function of providing a community within which the advantages of community living could be gained (Asad, 1983; Durkheim, 1912/1915; Troeltsch, 1931). Similar evidence abounds that even in recent times church members help

Contextualizing religion 131

each other out and provide exchanges, economic and otherwise, beyond what mere neighbours would provide (Child & Child, 1993; Hargrove, 1989; Wilson, 1988). Such social support through a church can be powerful in highly organized churches such as the Mormons, with the extreme being religious groups such as the Amish or Mennonites where life is lived completely within the church and contact with outsiders reduced.

On a smaller scale, showing the social basis of religious behaviour, anthropologists study how rituals and religious activities in tribes around the world change, sometimes in subtle ways, according to the social and political changes (Barth, 1987; Bloch, 1992; Evans-Pritchard, 1956; Firth, 1960; Geertz, 1973, p. 170). The earlier idea that rituals were static forms of behaviour (fixed structures) with never-changing repeated patterns has been overturned in these literatures (cf. Chapter 2).

The real question of religion, when seen in this light, becomes one of how social groups are organized for the many beneficial consequences of group participation and cooperation. Clearly, religious methods of group control or governance seem to differ from secular methods, but we will see later that there is a great deal of overlap between the two, or rather, that any group of people being shaped into a system of reciprocal consequences is usually shaped into using similar types of methods.

Contextualizing strategies for the social control of groups

So far, I have tried to show that while Pathway 1 analyses have been made of religion and religious behaviours, the real function *once contextualized* is to form, maintain, and govern groups of people so that cooperative benefits become available (Pathway 2). In this sense, ironically, money really *is* our current religion (as people sometimes might remark flippantly) since it is money that keeps our main social relationships going in modernity and that keeps us all cooperating at work (see Chapter 3).

I will now examine several types of religious behaviours and show *how they function to shape people into social groups*, rather than originating from 'within' people, and the individual 'internal' experiences 'causing' human behaviours. In each case, the Pathway 1 explanation of religious behaviour becomes reversed into Pathway 2.

Taboo

Taboos and taboo rituals about blood, handling corpses, and dangerous foods, are usually said to function because they help escape the anxiety associated with such activities (Douglas, 1966; Homans, 1941; Steiner, 1956). This Pathway 1 explanation can be argued in reverse, however; that *if these activities have strong aversive properties then they are perfect to use for shaping social control and managing groups.* Those who are shaping the social group can incorporate these already 'motivated' activities into social strategies to maintain control of a group by making their escape contingent upon completing other socially relevant, but lower-probability, activities. The taboo activities are particularly useful because they probably do not need regular maintenance, unlike positive shaping. So, this concurs with social anthropologists and sociologists who argue that taboo rituals are primarily for social control, not for any personal experiences (Durkheim, 1912/1915; Evans-Pritchard, 1965).

Such an argument is reflected in Radcliffe-Brown's (1952, p. 134) suggestion to call such behaviours 'ritual prohibition' or 'ritual avoidance'. His theory was that rituals and taboos serve to demonstrate the 'social value' of those events/objects: "Taboos relating to the animals and plants used for food are means of affixing a definite social value to food, based on its importance" (Radcliffe-Brown, 1952, p. 151). One implication of this is that those shaping the group should *promote* aversion to the taboo events rather than promote reduction of anxiety, because otherwise the 'power' (social consequences) of the social control will be lost. Riches (1994, p. 394), however, writes that: "I favour an alternative position, which is that cultural forms—taboos, systems of classification, or whatever—are sustained through the strategic work of individuals."

Rituals

The same contextualizing can be applied more generally to other religious rituals, that they function so that *regular contact with the social consequences can be maintained* (Guerin, 1992). In this sense, rituals provide an opportunity for monitoring the maintenance of social control, and so the more regular the ritual, the more accurate social monitoring will be. Similarly, conducting rituals publicly provide an opportunity for monitoring large groups of people.

So, it is argued that performing rituals does not enhance group solidarity or feelings of community because of the wonderful experiences thus obtained (Pathway 1), as suggested by Durkheim (1912/1915). Nor is it due to just the presence of symbols per se: "The primary basis of ritual ... is the attribution of ritual value to objects and occasions which are either themselves objects of important common interests linking together the persons of a community or are symbolically representative of such objects" (Radcliffe-Brown, 1952, p. 151). But why should attributing 'ritual value' to objects or occasions be important? Rather, it is suggested that the function of ritual is as a method to shape, influence, or organize the people of the community, and the 'valuable' objects and occasions serve instead to facilitate the shaping of behaviour. As we will see, there are strategic advantages to using objects or occasions that are artificially or socially given 'value'.

Totems

Totemism refers to a type of 'religious' behaviour in which groups have an animal or plant as their totem and must carry out various rituals in association with the name of the totem or the presence of the totem (Evans-Pritchard, 1965; Fortes, 1967; Lévi-Strauss, 1963b). For example, someone might be prohibited from killing the animal of their totem or must utter a ritual phrase when ever encountering that totem animal.

Durkheim argued that while totems function to keep groups together, a group requires *attachment* to common objects and ceremonials, and that people develop spiritual *affinities* and religious *sentiment* for the objects around them (amazingly Pathway 1 words in italics). He also argued that the reason for having animals and plants as a totem was that they could be put on to more permanent emblems and figures, and such emblems were important for totems. But, as Radcliffe-Brown (1952) pointed out, there are tribes that do not draw their totems or make statues of them at all.

Radcliffe-Brown (1952) himself argued that totems are part of ritual behaviours and everywhere people have *a special relationship to the animals and natural events around them* (Pathway 1 explanations again, beautifully mocked by Evans-Pritchard, 1965). Each moiety or clan then takes on one of these animals or natural events as its totem. The question for him therefore became: why do people adopt animals into their rituals? He suggested a general law: "Any object or event which has important effects upon the well-being (material or spiritual) of a society, or anything which stands for or represents any such object or event, tends to become an object of the ritual attitude" (Radcliffe-Brown, 1952, p. 129). This formulation, however, merely begs the question, whether the correlation is correct or not. It does not explain the cause or function of having animals as either totems or as part of a larger ritual attitude, nor why they tend to become an object of the ritual attitude.

These arguments have all assumed that the use of spiritual totems *reflects* a special *relation* between the individual person and their totem (like the false metaphorical 'special relation' between words and objects; see V1.3). Alternatively, a bit like words and art objects, totems can be viewed as *arbitrary* items that are used in social control strategies because they are (1) common, (2) accessible, and (3) easy to 'remember', and therefore more useful methods in long-term maintenance. As pointed out elsewhere (Guerin, 1994), a rarely sighted totem would only allow limited application of the social strategies to maintain the functioning groups and the cooperation and monitoring of social compliance or reshaping of the social organization (cf. Fortes, 1967, p. 17; Riches, 1994, p. 395).

It is suggested that shaping and monitoring of group cooperation is easier if objects and events with arbitrarily applied social consequences are used. Such symbols can set the occasion for compliance to a ritual behaviour—or monitoring whether the ritual was performed—and also for the reshaping of social organization during rituals (see Guerin & Ortolan, 2017, for similar control methods used by perpetrators of domestic violence control).

Mystification about the universe

The most frequent Pathway 1 claim for explaining religious behaviour (and religions use this frequently as well) is that humans are mystified and anxious about the universe, and that religion helps them come to terms with, or understand it (Freud, 1934). Some doubt about this reasoning has been voiced by Evans-Pritchard (1965), who reports that if you actually spend time with them, 'primitive' people are not, in fact, mystified by the universe and the meaning of life at all.

Looked at the shaping of groups of people, however, it can be argued that if puzzlement about the great questions of life *is* consequential for people, or is intentionally exaggerated and made to be consequential, then it can be *utilized* for gaining or maintaining social control in a group. People's puzzlement about the universe can be used in social contingencies as a source of power if answers and anxiety reduction are made contingent upon other, lower-probability, religious behaviours. Once again, if escape from such existential angst can be made contingent upon performing other religious and social behaviours, then social control of the group can be done in this way. And all this originates in people's external social world (Pathway 2), not inside them.

Some evidence for this argument comes from the implication that religions would therefore *promote* such mystification about the universe and life itself, rather than attempt to reduce it. If the members of a church were no longer puzzled and mystified about life, the universe, and everything, then this could not be utilized for social control. It is interesting, then, that most holy books *promote* this tendency and raise many questions about life and the universe that might not otherwise be asked. Indeed, this is a puzzling problem for the view that religions reduce anxiety about such mysteries: why would churches preach fire and brimstone, and raise questions of life and the universe? Would not it be better to keep quiet about all this?

The reversed Pathway 2 argument I have given suggests that the anxiety is *utilized* for organizing the social group rather than being reduced, and any induction of more anxiety therefore follows a Pathway 2 logic.

Personal crises and religious behaviour

Another input from psychology is the claim that religious experience occurs when people are unhappy, depressed, or in dire straits (James, 1902/1958) or personal crises, and that this somehow 'explains' the experiences. This is very Pathway 1 since it happens inside the individual person. Seen as social shaping (Pathway 2), however, alternative interpretations are possible. Like taboos and rituals, if someone is in a personal crisis then this is also the best condition for socially shaping their behaviour by making escape contingent upon performing religious behaviours. This same strategy will unfortunately shape those in control to *promote* personal crises in others to strengthen their religion.

A similar social strategy usually lies behind behaviours that are explained as 'catharsis', the expression of 'pent-up emotion', or release (e.g. Guerin, 2001; Kertzer, 1988, p. 131; see also Chapter 9). While the people involved are almost certainly angry or emotional beforehand and less so after such rituals and activities, the real question is why the ritual was organized in the first place. From a social control point of view the answer must look at what the people were required to do before their 'emotion' was expressed, released, or catharized; what was the low-probability behaviour?

Ambiguity

Ambiguity also allows for escape from social consequences (Middleton, 1977). If God is ineffable then priests and elders cannot be wrong about any interpretations of ambiguous scriptures or traditions. Keen (1994) highlights another social function of ambiguity, that religious ambiguity allows for variation and change in religious rituals and traditions so they can adapt to local social contingencies to help the group:

> It is perhaps not putting it too strongly to say that the ambiguity of religious and other forms of discourse entailed both variation and continual transformation: variation because the common shapes co-operatively produced were variously "read"; transformation because people could alter their readings of similar forms through time as well as differ, as between individuals and groups, and because those "forms" were the products of contexts.
> (Keen, 1994, p. 292)

Such ambiguities allow for continual social shaping in line with new social and resource exigencies. If rituals and religious behaviours were totally fixed, and this might never actually occur, tight social control would be necessary when the inevitable changes in the social and physical conditions occurred. Most religions, therefore, are usefully ambiguous with regards to authority and interpretation of scriptures (e.g. Harrison, 1959).

We also find an argument from Lévi-Strauss (1966) that myths and totems are formed from opposites or from some relation that produces many variations to 'think with' (Lévi-Strauss, 1963a). So, for each myth there will be related ones with the opposite relations (Sperber, 1979). From the present perspective, this would be a functional discursive strategy because, like ambiguity, it allows multiple controls over someone else's behaviour, especially when the social context changes.

Witchcraft

The anthropological literature has made it clear for many years that witchcraft and sorcery are also part of the social negotiation of social relationships and keeping groups working together, whenever they occur:

> Keeping our eyes fixed on the dynamic meaning of witchcraft, and recognizing therefore its universality, we shall better understand how it comes about that witches are not ostracized and persecuted ... confirmed witches known for miles around as such, live like ordinary citizens. Often they are respected fathers and husbands ... A witch may enjoy a certain amount of prestige on account of his powers, for everyone is careful not to offend him, since no one deliberately courts disaster. This is why a householder who kills an animal sends presents of meat to the old men who occupy neighbouring homesteads ... Likewise a man will be careful not to anger his wives gratuitously, for if one of them is a witch he may bring misfortune on his head by a bad fit of temper.
> (Evans-Pritchard, 1937/1976, p. 54)

Witchcraft does not pretend to be a primitive form of science but is a complex and sophisticated system of socially controlling groups of people (see Chapter 1). Like shamanism, it is important that the focus is on some individuals in a group who mediate the shaping and maintenance of the whole group, even if those persons are not controlling the group in a rule-governed or leadership role (Driver, 1991; Riches, 1994). Both are social phenomena for shaping the group to cooperate and reciprocate. Like the priests and ministers of larger organized religions, these smaller social systems also rely on social shapers such as witches and shamans.

Religious and non-religious behaviours?

The position so far is that when socially contextualized, religion is one very common form of organizing or shaping groups of people and has itself culturally grown through many and varied outcomes. These outcomes might be beneficial to the whole group or stratified to benefit just a few members of that group. The problem, then, is one of showing that the functions and explanations of religious behaviour given earlier in this chapter can be redefined as social control by groups, and to show how this can plausibly be shaped.

But if religious behaviours are one way of dealing with social situations, conflicts, cooperation, and exchange, this means that *the same social shaping could be carried out by means of secular solutions* (Gluckman, 1972; Moore & Myerhoff, 1977). This implies that there will be no clear division between religious and secular methods of shaping groups of people. In being opportunistic (not in the crass sense of the word) about how to shape groups of people, many variations become available and there is no firm divide between the strategies used in religious and non-religious forms of control. "The characteristic feature of this type of ritualization is that *it makes use of* the details of particular social relationships" (Gluckman, 1964, p. 120, my italics).

Similar views have been made before. First, overlap between the religious and secular is reflected in Evans-Pritchard's (1965) conclusions about theories of religion. Most theories, he argued, merely attempt to explain the origins of religious behaviours, for which we have no data but centuries of speculation. After reviewing and debunking all these theories he proposed no new theory of his own. The reason for this was that there *he found no clear divide between religious and non-religious activities.* Both are cultural activities that can control social behaviour in groups for cooperative outcomes. We can research the changes or dynamics of such social organizations, as Evans-Pritchard (1956) recommended, and we can investigate the conditions for religious solutions and their relative properties compared to non-religious solutions. In either case we must research the entire social situation and place religious behaviours within that context (Pathway 2).

> My test of this sort of formulation is a simple one: whether it can be broken down into problems which permit testing by observation in field research, or can at least aid in a classification of observed facts. I have never found that the dichotomy of sacred and profane was of much use for either purpose.
>
> (Evans-Pritchard, 1965, p. 65)

As an example of this, Geertz (1973, p. 142) reported on a funeral held in Central Java that was protracted and not effective. Parts of the rituals were changed and some parts were not followed. Geertz traced this to *both* religious differences *and* secular social unrest in the town, which had been developing for some time. If he had not known about the secular social conflicts in the groups he was studying, he would not have had an explanation for the changes made to the religious rituals he was observing.

The mixing of religious and non-religious social control methods can also be seen in Wilson's (1973) discussion of why new religious movements fail. All the reasons he gives for failure reflect the non-religious components in religions. For example, in some cases the new religious movements brought in too many non-religious elements, and because there was little institutionalization to keep the movement going, they failed. As another example, in 1968 the Catholic Church proclaimed, relying upon the papal infallibility that had likewise been proclaimed in July 1870, that birth control was condemned. This brought *a non-religious practice under religious control*, and many Catholics left the church at that point. The heavy institutionalization of this church, however, and its embeddedness in the everyday lives of its adherents, kept most members faithful, although papal infallibility had to be reaffirmed in July 1973.

Religion can therefore be seen as just one form of cultural shaping to control and develop cooperating groups of people. Once there is a community history of religion then it is usually easier to solve social conflicts and problems *religiously* than with *secular* strategies, if the majority of the group follow those religious practices. If there is no history of religion, then using religious strategies will usually fail.

Similar strategies in the secular world

In line with the earlier theme of this chapter, I hope it can be seen that in each of these cases of explanation reversal, there can be secular contexts that use the same strategies for similar social predicaments (Moore & Myerhoff, 1977). Religious solutions are not the only way to regulate a group, but historically they have been extremely important and continue to be so.

Secular rituals are well-known examples of similar strategies being used outside of religious contexts (Moore & Myerhoff, 1977). Bureaucracies regularly use strategies of secrecy and ambiguity to run those organizations, while team groups in sports will often take on a mascot as if a totem, although such mascots do not have the full 'significance' (social consequences) that totems have (Fortes, 1967).

It turns out, then, that there is little difference between religious and secular control of social groups, perhaps only the number of times various strategies are used or that religious groups usually, but not always, verbally propose a higher being or non-material existence (ambiguity). But the strategic use of ineffable, higher beings and non-material existences also occur in secular forms, for example, in the groups that have become organized around the existence of unidentified flying objects (UFOs) (Festinger, Reicken, & Schachter, 1956; Wallis, 1975a). They have also been increasingly utilized as Dianetics moved into becoming Scientology, from a type of psychotherapeutic cult to a more religious or spiritual organization (Wallis, 1975b).

Conclusions

In summary, what has been argued is that while Pathway 1 ideas led to explanations based on specific *internal and individual effects of religious behaviours*, a Pathway 2 analysis is that religious behaviours are just any behaviours that are shaped by 'religious' strategies to form and maintain a cooperative group for the large benefits this can produce. When we contextualize the *function* of religion and religious behaviours in this way, we can see the same ordinary life behaviours being used now within a secular context. The difference has to do with differences in how the religious and secular groups wield their strategies differently.

In V6.2, I will show a very similar occurrence of this pattern just summarized. It will be argued there that the real (Pathway 2) function of 'mental health' behaviours is to attempt to escape, avoid, or survive very bad life situations where alternative behaviours are blocked. This will lead to a similar conclusion that there are many other ways that people escape, avoid, or survive bad life situations, which are really no different in terms of this function, but that are not classified as 'mental health' issues. These include violence, drug taking, exploitation of others, and excessive control. Just as we can see that underlying the religious/secular dichotomy are the same ordinary behaviours that have been shaped differently but through the same functioning, so violent and criminal attempts to escape, avoid, or survive bad life situations only differ in how they are shaped *in situ* from 'mental health' behaviours and can be usefully treated as similarly functioning behaviours when we wish to change them.

Finally, this has only dealt with the broad picture of the major institutionalized religions. When we get to finer details and contextualizing more specific groups, we need to include a lot more. For example, more recent work on totems and animisms are finding amazing ways in which the gaps between doing things (to people) *with words* and doing other things to both animals and people *without words* (V1.7), and the variations on thinking, all play out (Brightment, Grotto, & Ulturhasheva, 2012; Costa & Fausto, 2010; Vilaça, 2010; Viveiros de Casto, 2015; Willerslev, 2007). There are also major differences between religious strategies to hold together kin-based communities and communities of strangers.

References

Asad, T. (1983). Anthropological conceptions of religion: Reflections on Geertz. *Man*, *18*, 237–259.
Barth, F. (1987). *Cosmologies in the making: A generative approach to cultural variation in inner New Guinea*. Cambridge, UK: Cambridge University Press.
Bloch, M. (1992). *Prey into hunter: The politics of religious experience*. Cambridge, UK: Cambridge University Press.
Brightment, M., Grotto, V. E., & Ulturhasheva, O. (Eds.) (2012). *Animism in rainforest and tundra: Personhood, animals, plants and things in contemporary Amazonia and Siberia*. New York, NY: Berghahn.
Child, A. B., & Child, I. L. (1993). *Religion and magic in the life of traditional people*. Englewood Cliffs, NJ: Prentice-Hall.
Costa, L., & Fausto, C. (2010). The return of the animists: Recent studies of Amazonian ontologies. *Religion and Society: Advances in Research*, *1*, 89–109.
Douglas, M. (1966). *Purity and danger*. New York, NY: Praeger.
Driver, T. E. (1991). *The magic of ritual*. San Francisco, CA: Harper & Row.
Durkheim, E. (1912/1915). *The elementary forms of the religious life: A study in religious sociology*. New York, NY: Macmillan.
Evans-Pritchard, E. E. (1956). *Nuer religion*. Oxford: Clarendon Press.
Evans-Pritchard, E. E. (1965). *Theories of primitive religion*. Oxford: Clarendon Press.
Evans-Pritchard, E. E. (1937/1976). *Witchcraft, oracles, and magic among the Azande*. Oxford: Clarendon Press.
Festinger, L., Riecken, H. W., & Schachter, S. (1956). *When prophecy fails: A social and psychological study of a modern group that predicted the destruction of the world*. New York, NY: Harper and Row.
Firth, R. (1960). The plasticity of myth. *Ethnologia*, *2*, 181–188.
Firth, R. (1996). *Religion: A humanist interpretation*. London: Routledge.
Fortes, M. (1967). Totem and taboo. In *Proceedings of the Royal Anthropological Institute of Great Britain and Ireland for 1966* (pp. 5–22). London: Royal Anthropological Institute.
Freud, S. (1934). *The future of an illusion*. London: Hogarth.
Geertz, C. (1973). *The interpretation of cultures*. New York, NY: Basic Books.
Gluckman, M. (1964). *Custom and conflict in Africa*. New York, NY: Barnes & Noble.
Gluckman, M. (1972). Moral crises: Magical and secular solutions. In M. Gluckman (Ed.), *The allocation of responsibility* (pp. 1–50). Manchester: Manchester University Press.
Guerin, B. (1992). Social behavior as discriminative stimulus and consequence in social anthropology. *Behavior Analyst*, *15*, 31–41.
Guerin, B. (1994). *Analyzing social behavior: Behavior analysis and the social sciences*. Reno, NV: Context Press.
Guerin, B. (2001). Replacing catharsis and uncertainty reduction theories with descriptions of the historical and social context. *Review of General Psychology*, *5*, 44–61.

Guerin, B., & Ortolan, M. O. (2017). Analyzing domestic violence behaviors in their contexts: Violence as a continuation of social strategies by other means. *Behavior and Social Issues, 26*, 5–26

Hamilton, M. B. (1995). *The sociology of religion: Theoretical and comparative perspectives*. New York, NY: Routledge.

Hargrove, B. (1989). *The sociology of religion: Classical and contemporary approaches* (2nd ed.). Arlington Heights, IL: Harlan Davidson.

Harrison, P. M. (1959). *Authority and power in the Free church tradition*. Princeton, NJ: Princeton University Press.

Homans, G. C. (1941). Anxiety and ritual: The theories of Malinowski and Radcliffe-Brown. *American Anthropologist, 43*, 164–172.

James, W. (1902/1958). *The varieties of religious experience: A study in human nature*. New York, NY: New American Library.

Keen, I. (1994). *Knowledge and secrecy in an Aboriginal religion*. Oxford: Clarendon Press.

Kertzer, D. I. (1988). *Ritual, politics, and power*. New Haven, CT: Yale University Press.

Lévi-Strauss, C. (1963a). The bear and the barber. *Journal of the Royal Anthropological Institute, 43*, 1–11.

Lévi-Strauss, C. (1963b). *Totemism*. Boston, MA: Beacon Press.

Lévi-Strauss, C. (1966). *The savage mind*. London: Weidenfeld & Nicolson.

Malinowski, B. (1925/1948). *Magic, science and religion, and other essays*. New York, NY: Free Press.

Middleton, J. (1977). Ritual and ambiguity in Lugbara society. In S. F. Moore & B. G. Myerhoff (Eds.), *Secular ritual* (pp. 73–90). Amsterdam: Van Gorcum.

Moore, S. F., & Myerhoff, B. G. (Eds.) (1977). *Secular ritual*. Amsterdam: Van Gorcum.

Nadel, S. F. (1957). Malinowski on magic and religion. In R. Firth (Ed.), *Man & culture: An evaluation of the work of Bronislaw Malinowski*. London: Routledge & Kegan Paul.

Radcliffe-Brown, A. R. (1952). *Structure and function in primitive society*. London: Cohen & West.

Riches, D. (1994). Shamanism: The key to religion. *Man, 29*, 381–405.

Sperber, D. (1979). Claude Lévi-Strauss. In J. Sturrock (Ed.), *Structuralism and since: From Lévi-Strauss to Derrida* (pp. 19–51). New York, NY: Oxford University Press.

Steiner, F. (1956). *Taboo*. Harmondsworth, UK: Penguin.

Tawney, R. H. (1938). *Religion and the rise of capitalism: A historical study*. New York, NY: Penguin Books.

Troeltsch, E. (1931). *The social teaching of the Christian churches*. London: Allen & Unwin.

Vilaça, A. (2010). *Strange enemies: Indigenous agency and scenes of encounters in Amazonia*. London: Duke University Press.

Viveiros de Castro, E. (2015). *The relative native: Essays on Indigenous conceptual worlds*. Chicago, IL: Hau Books.

Wallis, R. (1975a). The Aetherius Society: A case study in the formation of a mystagogic congregation. *Sociological Review, 22*, 27–44.

Wallis, R. (1975b). Scientology: Therapeutic cult to religious sect. *Sociology, 9*, 89–100.

Wikipedia (n.d.). Neuroscience of religion. Retrieved from https://en.wikipedia.org/wiki/Neuroscience_of_religion.

Willerslev, R. (2007). *Soul hunters: Hunting, animism and personhood among the Siberian Yukaghirs.* Berkeley: University of California Press.

Wilson, B. R. (1973). *Magic and the millennium: A sociological study of religious movements of protest among tribal and third-world peoples.* London: Heinemann.

Wilson, B. R. (1988). The functions of religion: A reappraisal. *Religion, 18*, 199–216.

9 Weaning yourself off social psychology

In Volume 4, I gave some tips for how you might stop thinking in terms of abstract, fictitious, 'cognitive' words, and, while not denying the 'cognitive' phenomena, find better and more observable ways to deal with them (V4.8). Here I want to briefly do the same with the social psychology literature.

There are several forms of 'social psychology' and in this chapter I am referring to the experimental cognitive forms prevalent in Western countries in the last few decades, heavily based on cognitive psychology and Pathway 1. In Brazil and elsewhere, what is labelled social psychology is very different and much more radical, community-based, and activist. Within sociology there is also another form labelled 'social psychology', which has some but not all the features I will outline in this chapter.

When I first started social psychology in my undergraduate years, there were actually two courses available and I did both. One was taught by an older lecturer and a lot was about precognitive models and theories of social behaviour, some based on observation of natural behaviour, and a little was linked to sociology (Allport, 1924; Cartwright & Zander, 1953; Murphy, Murphy, & Newcomb, 1931; Shaw & Constanzo, 1970). The second 'social psychology' course was by a younger, new lecturer, and while he knew the older material and a lot of sociology, this course was taught very much from a cognitive and experimental perspective (see Shaw & Constanzo, 1970, for an early version of this; Fiske & Taylor, 1984, was the 'bible' that appeared later).

It was only recently I remembered this and realized that I was there at a transition between two ways of doing social psychology. Both were Pathway 1, but the older version used a lot of everyday ways of explaining social behaviour as its basis and as its subject matter (response 3 to Pathway 1, V4.1). The newer version used cognitive models and metaphors of information processing and applied these to social phenomena (response 2), which still often used everyday descriptions to decide what counted as the phenomena. This was reflected in the common use (almost mandatory sometimes) of using pithy little everyday proverbs or sayings in the titles of journal papers, to indicate that these really were problems of life. Of the three ways that those on Pathway 1 proceed, only the brain route was not used back then (although social psychology is being overrun currently with 'brain explanations' of social behaviours based on correlations).

Contextualizing social psychology and methodologies

A problem with Western social psychology was that it not only employed very abstract and non-observable language for its models of 'phenomena', but the methods for studying these 'phenomena' were also exceedingly abstract and context-free. Most, as we will see in what follows, were only ever studied by participants *talking* about the phenomena or answering abstract questions about the phenomena (now done in online surveys), and they were very rarely observed *in situ*, that is, in context. Some were in fact completely fictitious and there was no *in situ* (including my own doctoral research; cf. Guerin, 1993, 2001a) The discipline has also heavily relied on other abstract notions such as 'personality' to sustain its research, and even these 'personality' features can usually *only* be measured through the participants writing answers to questions, and treating those answers as realistic descriptions of something.

What this means is that a portion of the social psychological 'findings' cannot be rescued as observable phenomena in context that merely need a rethinking or contextualizing. It takes time and effort to tell the difference.

The main ideas of this form of social psychology mostly came from combining responses (2) and (3) to the Gestalt problem via Pathway 1 (V4.1): (2) uses abstract models and simulations to guess what is going on inside the brain, and (3) uses everyday common ideas and treat them as descriptions of the phenomena and as the subject matter that needs to be studied. Most recently this has not been working well and so the first response is now increasingly prevalent: (1) explain all the 'social' phenomena in terms of hypothesized brain and physiology mechanisms.

To their credit, over my decades of working in social psychology, there have been many attempts to criticize the discipline and to change it (e.g. Armistead, 1974; Doise, 1986; Gough, McFadden, & McDonald, 2013; Harré & Secord, 1972; Lana, 1991; Moscovici, 1961/2008; Potter, 1996; Tajfel, 1984; Tuffin, 2004). Ironically, the main catchphrase has always been to 'put the social back into social psychology' (cf. Chapter 1). It has long been clear to many, therefore, that cognitive social psychology was no longer dealing with actual social behaviour but only with 'perceptions of' or 'talking about' social behaviour and treating these as real. Each of these critical attempts is based on criticizing the two Pathway 1 responses mentioned above: that abstract models of what might be happening replace the actual social behaviour, and the excessive use of everyday terms about social behaviour substituting for good descriptions of social behaviour.

These both became worse when fuelled by using cognitive theories as the basis for human social behaviour, and this use of cognitive theories relied on W. I. Thomas and the mistaken idea that our thinking causes our behaviour (see later in the chapter and V4.4): *if we can study how people cognize or think about social phenomena (gleaned from everyday talk), then this is also how people control and decide their social behaviour.* Surely?

In my experience, the only good attempt to really change all this thinking and research in social psychology was through the later introduction of discourse analysis to traditional social psychology (e.g. Edwards, 1997; Edwards & Potter, 1992, 1993; Potter, 1996; Potter & Edwards, 1990; Potter, Wetherell, & Chitty, 1991; Putcha & Potter, 2002; Wetherell & Potter, 1992). All previous attempts to be critical merely went back to the same assumptions in new forms. There were also many people I knew personally who left the field altogether to go into health psychology and other domains because they could see the problems.

The main assumptions of social psychology that need rethinking

I will go through several of the main ideas used in social psychology (Pathway 1) and then outline how we might take a social contextual view of what is going on (Pathway 2) and merge with the social sciences. In terms of the title of this book, notice how in each case we merge the study of social behaviour back in line with sociological and social anthropological ideas about people and social worlds. For example, Serge Moscovici (1961/2008) made a great attempt (drawing on Durkheim) to take this path by talking about 'social representations' being *part of* discursive societies and wider society (I learned a lot from him for V4.3). But ultimately, this approach became the study of how 'social representations' were stored in an individual's memory and cognitively processed, an interpretation on which Moscovici was always ambiguous. My view is that it was not really about whether he did or did not believe the cognitive interpretation, but rather, as I suggested for Marx and ideology in Chapter 6, Moscovici wanted a Pathway 2 version but simply did not know how to do this.

1. Individualistic

From its earliest conception (the modern psychological forms), the vision of social psychology has been based on a very individualistic notion of 'human', borrowing from the dominant economic forms of 'rational man' (Siedentop, 2004; see also Chapter 1). We are all self-contained organisms who decide or choose our own fate while being affected by external forces. Any changes in behaviour are brought about by internal changes; our behaviour originates or is created internally, usually in our thinking. *'Social' behaviour is therefore about two self-contained organisms doing things to each other by individually deciding.* Even when overwhelmed by emotions, this is about some *internal* emotional responses overwhelming the 'rational' person in a Humean way.

In the words of one of the founders of modern Western social psychology:

> There is no psychology of groups which is not essentially and entirely a psychology of individuals. Social psychology must not be placed in contradistinction to the psychology of the individual; *it is part of the psychology of the individual*, whose behavior it studies in relation to that sector of his environment comprised by his fellows ... Behavior, consciousness, and organic life belong strictly to individuals; but there is surely occasion for speaking of the group as a whole so long as we do not regard it as an organism or a mental entity.
>
> (Allport, 1924, pp. 4, 10, italics in original)

Certainly, we do *not* want to think of a group of people as another organism nor as a mental entity; we can deny the individualism without then having to think of a group of people as having a 'group mind'. So, what are the problems here?

- These paragraphs mix up individual, internal, cause, behaviour, and control. A billiard ball moves around as a single unit and we do not want to think that a *group* of billiard balls has a super-mind, but this does *not* mean that they cannot be completely controlled *externally*.
- 'Consciousness' (as we saw in V4) is usually used to refer to talking that is not said out loud, but this, like the billiard balls, is controlled externally by discursive communities. This manoeuvre allows Allport (and everyone since until discourse analysis) to assume that the talk used in deciding or choosing behaviour must originate inside a person as an individual and not in their external language communities; and that this internal talk is then said to be the cause of their behaviour.
- It wrongly assumes that the individuals have all been assembled independently of their social environments and only *then* do they go about 'deciding' things, interacting, being social. But this is false, and whenever an individual acts, this already *is* the social world acting! Our 'individual' behaviours are already external social actions (see Chapter 3)

since we are not 'assembled' independently of everything and only then thrown into the social arena.

As we have seen throughout, and especially for mental health (V6.2), the problem is that human social and societal shaping is usually hidden from us. If we hid away from your view the group of people shooting the billiard balls (you could not see them), it would certainly look to you like each ball was a 'self-propelled' decision maker. With language use, social behaviour, and societal shaped behaviour, we rarely see directly how the behaviours we do have been shaped or socially 'propelled'.

As we saw in V4.2, Allport's typical Pathway 1 vision of psychology, now applied to social psychology, allows theorists to invent or construct any manner of internal events that originate or 'cause' whatsoever the 'individual' does. This is like saying that (after being hit), the behaviour of the billiard ball can be explained internally (mass, acceleration, etc.). That is fine up to a point, but if we do not include the original external hitting of the ball in our observations, then when the ball stops we must predict that it will never act again. We have to have this awkward period in which the ball starts moving again, but we have not seen that someone hit the ball (this is hidden remember). We then explain that (1) the ball decided internally to move because it likes to, (2) balls move because they must hit other balls to survive and this is built into their DNA, (3) balls move because the previous hitting made it more probable that it would move again, or (4) our theory (fiction) of ball behaviour postulates that we can think of them as having an internal processing unit (like a computer!) which makes it move if that is what it computes based on its processing of previous hitting. If you do not do the contextual observations of the ball being externally hit originally by a bunch of people with sticks, then you miss the whole picture.

2. *Verbal reports substituted for social behaviour*

Most of recent social psychology in the Anglo-Saxon countries relies (too) heavily on participant verbal reports to substitute for all and any behaviour. Within social psychology (both in sociology and psychology) this is often uncritically 'supported' or casually justified by a statement of W. I Thomas: "If men define situations as real, they are real in their consequences" (Thomas & Thomas, 1928, pp. 571–572). But with the present approach and most discursive approaches, this does not really make sense. If I perceive that I am king of England, this does not make that reality. And my 'thinking' or 'defining' that I am king of England has already been shaped by my social world, but that is shaping my talking, not my 'being' the king of England. These can be independent.

This is yet another example of the Gestalt 'triangle' problem (V4.1), which mistakenly led to all the Pathway 1 psychologies for 60 years. If someone says, "I see a triangle", then are there real consequences? Well, yes and no. There are no real consequences for 'perceiving' the triangle (as when drawing it) but there are *social* consequences for what has been said. From V4.4, we need to reword Thomas thus: "If people define [talk about] situations as real, there may be real consequences from their social-discursive worlds but not from the objects they described." If I claim that "my cat is blue" then there *can* be consequences from anyone hearing this but claiming this in no way affects my cat or any other cat.

Using language is certainly important in everyday social life but this is different. By wrongly assuming that thoughts control our behaviour (see Chapter 5), researchers can assume that what people say they 'perceive' as the situation really *is* the situation (à la Thomas). And if people give verbal *reasons* why they do what they do, these uncritically become the 'true explanations'. I have gone through the problems with these assumptions in many places (e.g. V4.3, V4.7), and also with taking people's 'explanations' at face value, as if they are 'screen dumps' of the what is truly going on.

Better approaches have been put forward by various discourse analysis proponents (e.g. Edwards & Potter, 1993; Mills, 1940; Putcha & Potter, 2002) and less successfully by Skinner (1957). As summarized in Volume 4, talking and thinking are themselves behaviours requiring analysis and contextualizing, and they are shaped externally in our discursive worlds, so verbal reports cannot substitute for contextual observations.

Further problems with the excessive reliance on what people say arise from most of the 'pitfalls' of language use given in Volume 4, along with further problems with the common cognitive models used by most social psychologists nowadays (see also Edwards, 1997).

3. Little context is taken into account

Relying heavily on the explanations and descriptions people give about what and why they do things (as if that was tapping into the internal 'cause'), also has the problem of allowing social psychologists to avoid *observing* the behaviours being talked about and, more importantly, to ignore descriptions of the contexts for these behaviours. This would be like interviewing (or more likely via an online questionnaire) a billiard ball after the game in another room and asking, "So what motivates you to move and hit the other balls?" The billiard ball might say, "Well, I do not see anything around me but it feels like I just have to move forwards sometimes and hit other balls. I must like doing this." This means the researcher does not have to go and watch the game to report on the full context that also involves human players.

4. Psychologists have been varying contexts and the consequences of behaviour all along, but in hidden ways

Most social psychology research varies some real conditions experimentally or else, more usually, varies what individual participants are 'told' about the imagined conditions. As just mentioned, usually some form of talk is then recorded as the outcome of 'social' behaviour. So, participants might receive an essay to review, and some are told that it was written by a professor of psychology and others that it was by a high school student. They are then asked to rate the essay on some questionnaire dimensions with scales to tick.

Treated as language use or discourse, there is nothing wrong with this. But Thomas kicks in here because it is assumed that if participants *perceive* the writer as a professor then that is the reality for them. But this raises more questions than it can answer. Why should they believe that it is written by a professor? Because the experimenter told them? Do they trust the experimenter? A more likely problem is, *do they have any other alternative way to act or to believe what is going on here?* Are there any real consequences for the participants if they just go along with the experimenter's story? No, it is all abstract words and questionnaire ratings and they do not get punished for getting this wrong.

So, all the real contexts of rating this essay that might occur 'normally' are absent. The usual answer to this by social psychologists is to make it 'consequential' for participants by (again) *telling* them that their ratings of both this essay and the writer will likely mean that the writer will fail a course, for example. But this is still just a further *discursive* exercise for the participants. Not only are there reputed consequences for the writer of the essay but also consequences for going along with the experimenter's new story or not. And what alternatives do the participants have? They have no alternative story about the essay. Any real context is missing. And they cannot just exit. This is identical to Gibson's critique of most perception research—all the context is removed and so what they find is nothing like the everyday behaviour they are supposed to be studying (V4.5).

Sometimes social psychologists have tried harder to look at social behaviour that has 'real' consequences, even though many of these are still just stories fed to the participants and are only 'real' if you believe Thomas. Many years ago, I took the ten most prominent of these experimental manipulations of laboratory 'social' behaviour and found that they did seem to work (Guerin, 1991, 1994), but only because (1) they were all hiding some social consequences, and (2) participants had no alternative but to play along. Most were verbal manipulations of purported 'real' social consequences, but we have little idea what was really happening (V4.7).

The following were the ten manipulations I found reviewing the social psychology literature:

- *Future interaction*: the first type of manipulation assured (verbally) the participants that there would be some future interaction with the other people in the experiment, in order to vary social consequences. In such experiments, participants were told that they will have to meet the people they are interacting with, evaluating, or discussing, in future sessions. Participants in control conditions were either told that they will not be meeting the people again or else they were told nothing. The implicit assumption seems to be that the person to be met can give negative consequences to the participants in the later session, depending upon how they behaved in the first session.
- *Real consequences*: a second manipulation used some 'real' consequences that participants could gain or lose during interaction with others in experiments. For example, participants in the experimental condition might gain real money or they might make suggestions that will be used by the experimenter for real purposes. Most were verbally mediated and not direct, despite being called 'real'.
- *Explanations*: in a third manipulation it is stressed to participants that they must *explain* their behaviour afterwards, or give an account, either to the experimenter or to the other participating subjects. This implicitly meant that retribution, reward, evaluation, or other consequences, could have been made afterwards contingent upon performance.
- *Dependency*: another manipulation of consequences made participants 'responsible' for other participants, by having the other person dependent in some way upon the participants. Some studies had the others dependent on the real participants for rewards. Most of these studies used role playing and language-based techniques rather than real money, however.
- *Anonymity*: some studies have manipulated anonymity in various ways, telling participants that their results were confidential, private, or unidentifiable. If done carefully, this was supposed to guarantee that there will be no interpersonal consequences since individual results are not known. Many studies have done this through 'public' and 'private' conditions. All this still depends on trusting what the experimenter says and having no alternative stories available in the experimental context.
- *Responsibility*: consequences have also been manipulated by directly changing how responsible participants 'feel' for their behaviour. For

example, half the participants might be told that whatever they did, the experimenter would be responsible for anything that happened or went wrong. To what extent participants believed such manipulations is not known but will depend on verbal compliance with the experimenter and lack of an alternative story for participants.

- *Evaluation*: evaluation has also been used as a manipulation of accountability and consequences. Participants in this case do *not* have to explain their behaviour, but rather, other persons will evaluate their behaviour afterwards (or so they are told). Although these others may not be able in every case to proportion 'real' consequences afterwards, the assumption was that there was enough anxiety in being evaluated to suggest that it has important verbally mediated consequences for most participants.
- *Status*: a number of experimental social psychology studies have used manipulations that affect the participants' status with respect to the experimental group. Participants are told they may be trusted or not trusted, may have role obligations, or may have their jobs in jeopardy. With lower status, it has been argued that they are less accountable to the others so there can be less consequences. Once again, all this is constructed through verbal manipulations.
- *Reversibility*: a further manipulation of consequentiality was the reversibility of a decision or behaviour. If a behaviour with possible negative consequences can be reversed in the future, before negative consequences arise, this was said to mean less responsibility. In line with this, some experiments varied whether or not participants were able to change their decisions or behaviour after making an initial choice.
- *Control*: in this last manipulation, control of the consequences is given to another person to reduce the 'perceived' possible consequences. The participants do not have control of things in the situation except by altering their behaviour to influence the controller.

There are many problems with these experimental manipulations. Foremost, as I have detailed, are the assumptions that (1) verbal manipulations of 'real' consequences are the same as the actual real consequences à la Thomas, and that (2) 'thought controls our behaviour' (V4.4; see also Chapter 6). I have emphasized that these Pathway 1 assumptions go through *most* of what social psychology does in research.

A second problem is that real life allows diversity and negotiations in all of these types of social consequences, which are missing from the research. The real situations are not observed or studied systematically. What shapes human behaviour in real life has not been studied, just a verbal substitute. The participants are told that "their ratings of both this essay and the writer will likely mean that the writer will fail a course". But this is just talk, and they have *no alternative options or stories* to deal with or negotiate this other than just to play along.

5. Abstract surrogates are used in lieu of proper observations

Another pitfall of language use is that abstractions can seem like reality (V4.7). In lieu of observing real social behaviours in context, social psychologists have used a mixture of abstractions. The most common are 'personality variables' and rating scales divided into those who score high or low. So, participants might be divided into those high or low in 'self-esteem' based on a standardized questionnaire, rather than the researchers observing and describing the behaviours they are aiming to understand. Other examples include measuring beliefs, attitudes, roles, etc.

6. Thoughts control behaviour

Because they rely so much on participants' self-reports, which are assumed to be their personal 'inner' thoughts guiding their 'inner decisions' and 'perceptions', there is a strong reliance in social psychology on the idea that thoughts control our behaviour. This was all debunked in V4.4, Chapter 6 in this volume, and elsewhere by many social science writers. Once this is gone, a lot of social psychology no longer has a logic, and this includes other words such as 'intentions', which try and substitute for 'internal' control (for example in the belief models of Fishbein & Ajzen, 1975).

7. Cognition is opposed to emotions

Another common assumption within psychology and everyday life, also debunked in V4.6, is that our 'emotions' arise from inside us and they are opposed to, and can override, our thinking and rational thought. That is, we normally use thought to control our behaviour, but in some social situations our 'emotions' well up inside and we then stop acting 'rationally'. As we saw in Chapter 1, such reasoning has a long history and David Hume probably wrote the most clear form of this, albeit wrong.

8. The context has been assumed to be white, male, middle class, and Western

Though no longer completely true, the history of social psychology has assumed the context of a typical Western, middle-class population and their social behaviours. The whole field is based on typical *stranger or contractual interactions* and all of the social properties we have seen that are specific to such social relationships (see Chapter 3). Most of the 'universal' findings of social psychology as seen in textbooks would simply not replicate if they were instead conducted with poor, Indigenous, or kin-based populations, etc. This both arises from, and maintains, the individualistic assumptions made in social psychology. The usual response from social psychology, like the DSM, is to make 'cultural effects' a special category, rather than do a contextual analysis of what is really different across diverse groups, which does not single out 'cultural' groups.

9. Rules govern our behaviour

There is another solution for dealing with the contradictions involved when basing everything on language uses ('perceived situations', 'decisions', 'preferences') but treating them as good descriptions that can substitute for going out and observing in the person's world. This follows the (wrong) idea that words have the power to make people do things (V4.3, V4.7; see also Chapter 1), rather than the 'power' coming from real social events of social exchange and reciprocity over time.

Following some sociologists, this was often done by assuming that there are 'social norms' in any society and that people follow them because … well, just because. No one went out and observed what was happening in context (see Chapter 3). Another version, going back to Wittgenstein, was to assume there are 'rules' (replacing the 'social norms'), and that people are 'basically' rule followers (except when there are exceptions of course). This probably also mimicked the idea of computer software following a series of rules or instructions (V4.1), but the 'power' of any words to affect people was never observed (Douglas, 1973).

The main problem with these lines of reasoning was dealt with in Chapter 2 (and V4.4). That when functioning is repetitive then it begins to look like there is a fixed 'object-thing' that can predict behaviour. In the present case, if we have a very authoritarian society run by rules, then yes, it looks like the rules themselves have the power to make people do things, because everyone obeys. We put up speeding signs of 40 kph and people slow down. However, this ignores that the structure is just repetitive functioning and when that changes, the rules will no longer work. For those trying to govern, the solution is usually to make greater punishments for not following rules, whereas they should be investigating why people are no longer happy to follow the rules, or what functioning of human life is being left out.

10. Methodology without context

Finally, as we have seen in several cases, taking a Pathway 1 response to the Gestalt problem (V4.1) leads to the use of particular research methodologies that unfortunately are easier than the methodologies required by following Pathway 2. The same criticisms were made about traditional psychology by both Gibson and Skinner.

The main research point is not about qualitative versus quantitative, or experimental versus non-experimental, but about how we must describe the real external contexts for human actions, talking and thinking, *before* trying to develop or answer any research questions. I will break this into three main points.

How to document context to understand human actions, talking, and thinking?

In turning psychology into a social science, we luckily do not have to invent new contextual methodologies (Guerin, 2018; Guerin, Leugi, & Thain, 2018). Social anthropology and some sociology (and some ethology and ecology) have been developing contextual methodologies almost before psychology began. The main points are as follows:

- Document as much of the context for your research as possible, including (even for 'psychological problems') economic, patriarchal, and other societal contexts (see Chapter 3).
- Spend much more time doing this than traditional psychological methodologies.
- As far as you are allowed, *participate* in life with those who you are trying to understand.
- With respect to talking, allow the participants to lead the talking, they are the experts.
- Treat any talking as discourse and not as de facto descriptions of 'facts'.
- Keep the full contexts *in situ* because once you reduce normal context (for experimental manipulations) you do not know what you are dealing with any longer.

Research outcomes as talk or action?

Another change to research methodologies (and clinical interventions as it turns out; see V6) from taking Pathway 2, is that we only really find out anything by changing the world and seeing what happens. Again, both Skinner and Gibson remarked on this.

This is reflected in whether the goal of 'science' is changing the world or finding ways to talk about the world 'truthfully'. Most philosophies (Guerin, 2016) and psychologies are based on the latter, and believe we are trying to construct the best theories *to describe* how things truly work. The problem here goes back to misunderstanding the function of language and theories (V4.3). Any 'scientific' theory (words or equations) only affects the behaviour of other people, presumably other scientists, to get them to do something differently. 'Scientific" theories do not in any sense 'encapsulate' truth. As I have argued (V4.3), truth and falsity are never properties of words.

Research as social behaviours

A bigger change to research methodologies from following Pathway 2 is that we need to view *research itself as just social relationships*. This means it is shaped by all the different contexts of life, including societal ones (see Chapter 3). There is nothing special or 'extra-material' about the contexts for doing research, they are still just real life. The difference is in what exactly the researchers are doing to the participants, and how they arrange the research context.

Table 9.1 includes some suggestions of what can happen in such research contexts. Like all lists and tables in these books, they are there to sensitize

Table 9.1 Different research methodologies contextualized as social relationships

Types of research methodologies	Contextualizing the research social relationship
Laboratory research	Person out of the normal contexts that shape their behaviour
	Can be less of a problem if language use only is being measured (= cognition) since immediate control not needed
	Most alternative behaviours are excluded (e.g. cannot simply exit)
Experimental research	Often restrictions on 'normal' contexts are required even outside laboratories, so behaviour is out of the normal shaping contexts
Survey research questionnaires	What we be answered will depend upon a short-term stranger social relationship developed quickly with few consequences for whatever answers are given
	With few consequences for whatever is said (researcher and respondent not likely to meet ever again) this theoretically could lead to freer answering, but respondents are unlikely to trust this

(*continued*)

Table 9.1 Cont.

Types of research methodologies	Contextualizing the research social relationship
	If the 'beliefs' and 'attitudes' requested are not already generic ones, but specific and flexible according to the respondent's different normal social relationships, then some amalgam will be forged on the spot since this is an unknown audience being talked to
	No time to establish parameters for anything beyond a total stranger social relationship
Online or posted questionnaires	Many of the above points apply again
	Closed questions often do not match the experience or contexts of the respondents so answers will be an amalgam
Closed interviewing	Closed questions often do not match the experience or contexts of the respondents so answers will be an amalgam
	Usually assumes that respondents have one 'true' answer 'inside' and that having a neutral stranger is more likely to get that response, whereas responding is more of a function of different contexts and different to the usual audiences in their life
	Closed questions also typically cross over different audiences for the respondents so they might give one of their answers or a vague amalgam (or what they think the stranger wants)
	While time is sometimes allocated to 'building rapport' this will be inadequate to change from a stranger or contractual social relationship
	'Rapport building' is mutual and the respondent is also being shaped by what is said and done towards certain ways of responding
Open-ended interviewing	While similar to the above, letting the respondent answer more freely does not guarantee 'more truthful' answers, since they still do not have one of their usual audiences for their responses present
	Anything not within the scope of the themes or questions is usually vetoed since there is limited time, and the respondent brought back on task
Evaluation research	Similar to the above but the context also has consequences for other people and programmes, which again does not necessarily mean the responding will be 'truer'
	'Rapport building' is mutual and the respondent will be shaped by what is said about the impact of the outcomes

Table 9.1 Cont.

Types of research methodologies	Contextualizing the research social relationship
Focus groups	Many times, it has been pointed out how focus groups are about the social relationships of all involved but little has been changed because of this, just ignored If you are studying the interaction itself as discourse analysis this is fine, but emphasizes how 'normal' focus groups can shape the participants and we will not know
Action research	Varies depending upon whether the participants are seen frequently for non-stranger social relationships to develop There is a goal for action research and this might affect participants in different ways that will not be known Sometimes carried out in meeting rooms out of the participant's usual contexts Sometimes carried out in the participant's usual contexts More of a friend or acquaintance social relationship when time is spent with the participants, with the associated social properties
Participatory research	More chance for a stronger relationship that does not necessarily give 'truer' answers but probably more variations on a person's 'standard' answers that are given to strangers More time spent means actions and talking can be observed in different contexts, so the changes can be noted
Longitudinal research (repeated cross-sectional)	Some longitudinal research is like participatory research but much of it is really repeated cross-sectional research On repeated waves, even if just a survey is given, there may be a little more to the social relationship (and a shift in social properties therefore) since there is a slight history
Discourse analysis	Discourse analysis should include observations and detail of many of the participants' life contexts, especially their social relationships, although this is frequently left out Requires a thorough contextual analysis to make sense of what is being said or written Often of short duration, however, which means that participants and researchers do not develop beyond a stranger relationship

the readers for future observations, not to provide any sort of exhaustive or complete documentation. Language cannot even do that (V4.7).

Contextualizing some examples of important ideas in social psychology

The examples that follow are mostly cases where we can assume that there is a real phenomenon occurring and it is not all disguised verbal. These can be rescued but need to be contextualized and made sense of in that way (V2).

Cognitive biases

These have been dealt with in Volume 4 and Chapter 1 of this volume. 'Cognitions' are pieces of discourses shaped by all our discursive worlds and for various reasons are not said out loud (Table 4.1). They are socially based and external, therefore, and not 'in the head'. When social psychologists and others talk about 'cognitive *biases*' what they mean is that people are not doing what gains most resources, but in doing this they only look at the immediate and non-social 'resources' (see Chapter 1).

So, the ('cognitive') biases in fact appear because there are other hidden social, community, or societal outcomes that also determine what people say and do. The trick is not to conclude that biases show that human internal functioning is weak or dysfunctional, but that the person is actually smart by taking into account the social outcomes of what they are doing and not just the immediate non-social outcomes.

For example, if given a choice between $10 or $50, the obvious choice is the latter (if you only look at the immediate and non-social outcomes). But in numerous social situations this would look bad (have bad social outcomes) since it shows anyone observing that (1) you are greedy, (2) you have not considered that taking it all means someone else will get less, and (3) since the whole choice is (socially) suspicious in the first place. Taking the social outcomes into account is actually rational!

Cognitive dissonance

Cognitive dissonance (Festinger, 1957) suggested that when people have contradictory beliefs (in their minds, Pathway 1) this is aversive, and they will therefore act to change the situation. I have written about this elsewhere (Guerin, 2001b) and reanalysed some of the original classic research situations. I suggested that it be relabelled 'social dissonance' (if a label is even important) since hidden social contexts are producing the behaviours found.

Contextually, if a person 'has' contradictory beliefs this means they have two different discursive communities that are maintaining the two opposite beliefs (cf. Chapter 4). 'Having' the beliefs simply means that in context the person will say one or the other (depending on which discursive community is present at the time usually). This in itself is not aversive, not a problem, and extremely common. What is a problem for the person is when the contexts overlap in various ways, such as when your two communities are present at the same time (normally you would keep quiet).

In such ways, the original experiments in social psychology only worked because the experimenter surreptitiously (but on purpose) *got the participants* to believe something *contradictory* to normal beliefs. But the hidden discursive community in this case was the experimenters themselves, because they *hid* their influence on participants by trying to get participants to also believe that *they* had come up with that belief themselves. So they convinced them of a belief that was contradictory to common sense, and then disguised their role in making them believe this!

In one of the classic paradigms for studying cognitive dissonance, the *forced compliance* paradigm, Festinger and Carlsmith (1959) had participants do a very boring task in a laboratory. After the participants had done this, they were asked how much they enjoyed the original (boring) task they had done, and they all said that they all found it very boring. Then the experimenter *convinced* the participants to tell the next participant that the experiment was actually interesting, even though it patently was not. In a nice twist, the experimenters paid the participants either a very small amount of money or a large amount of money for lying to the next participant. They were then asked again how much they enjoyed the original (boring) task they had done. What they found was that those being paid a small amount changed their ratings to say they (retrospectively) enjoyed the task more than those who had been paid a large amount to lie.

The Pathway 1 reasoning was this: that those paid a small amount to lie had no obvious reason for why they lied to the next participant (since our internal reasons cause us to behave if you are on Pathway 1, and there was not a good reason in this case). They were presumably morally opposed to lying but they did it, for an amount *that could not justify* what they had done. Those paid the larger amount for lying did not change their 'cognitive beliefs' that the task was boring; although they also lied, they had a *sufficient justification* (the larger sum of money) and so there was no noxious cognitive dissonance present in their case and hence no change in attitudes or behaviour to reduce the dissonance.

There are some little-noticed peculiarities about such 'cognitive' dissonance situations, however. First, the social influence involved in getting participants to lie in the first place is surreptitious and no details are given in the methods section of the paper. But how *did* the experimenters persuade participants to tell the next person that the (boring) task was interesting when they had already told the experimenter it was not? This was a huge contextual social influence in this situation, but it is glossed over and does not get mentioned in the researchers' explanations for what had just happened! But that particular social context turns out to be the key to the whole experiment. It was a hidden social influence in the situation that probably controlled everything that happened later.

Looking even more closely at the context here, the experimenter in all this has said one thing and done another—the experimenter has been *dishonest* to the participants and the only reason that this was *not* used as a justification ("I told a lie because the experimenter made me do it") by participants was precisely because the experimenters were careful to let the participants think that *they themselves* chose to lie to the next participant (Festinger & Carlsmith, 1959).

If anything, these situations are indicative of 'social' dissonance rather than 'cognitive' dissonance. The dissonance is in having to explain socially and verbally some contradictory behaviours or attitudes to other people. If people lose sleep over dissonance it will be because they might have to explain what they did to a hostile audience, not because the 'brain' cannot stand having contradictory, dissonant elements inside of it. There is no 'inner anxiety' driving the outcome but two conflicting 'social influences' coming directly from the external social context (outside the person):

- An experimenter persuading the person to lie to the next participant but keeping this social influence carefully hidden so it could not be used as a justification by them later.
- Society telling the person that they should never lie and the next participant potentially accosting them at a later time because they had been lied to.

While there is not the space to deal with them in detail here, the other forms of cognitive dissonance manipulations involve the manipulation of verbal justifications, explanations, and storytelling that can be recontextualized in a similar way to the earlier discussion of social representation and social constructionism theories using conversational analysis. Once again, I am not arguing that these phenomena do not exist, just that the Pathway 1 explanations do not help us. Like the Gestalt triangle (V4.1), we must look at *all* the events in the context and include them all in our analyses.

Beliefs and attitudes

Beliefs and attitudes have been a major part of social psychology since its inception, but always following Pathway 1. As described better in Chapter 4, beliefs are just things we say in context to do things to people. This needs a discursive analysis of the social contexts in which we use belief statements and the outcomes of using them. When you hear people talking about beliefs and what they believe (including social psychologists), always look for the *social relationship contexts* that are maintaining these discourses. It does not matter if the beliefs seem true or false. Find out what they are being used to do to other people, and who these people are (perhaps not the listeners). And saying beliefs can function to oppose people as much as bond with them.

The same applies to attitudes. The only difference really is that attitudes hedge the discourses around beliefs (Guerin, 1994). Saying an attitude is rhetorically safer than saying a belief.

Attribution and attribution biases

Similarly, we do not have a *need* to understand and explain things around us, as many social psychologists claim (Guerin, 2001b, V4.3). People make explanations and give attributions *as part of doing things to people— doing their social behaviours* (Edwards & Potter, 1993). They are useful forms of discourse in many situations, whether to keep someone quiet or to manage your self-image to those around you. The different categories of attributions that social psychologists have usefully explored (consensus, attributions to internal or external factors, distinctiveness, and consistency) are just different rhetorical properties that usually give different outcomes for making the attributions (Edwards & Potter, 1993).

Social and personal identity

Social and personal identities are just surrogate internal ways of saying that people are important to all that humans do (see Chapter 5). All our resources come from people whether strangers or family, and how we present ourselves therefore changes our outcomes. These do not consist of some core 'inner person' but in the very acting out of all our behaviours. We are shaped by all those around us, including strangers, and also from society itself and the structures that are in place before we are even born. So, while the main point of 'self' is certainly correct and important, approaching this as a series of internal cognitive processes around managing 'self' (whatever form it might be) is less than helpful. We need to observe the contexts as they are rather than abstractly treating them as internal surrogates.

Obedience and Milgram (1974)

This is a famous experiment in social psychology but usually analysed in misleading ways. A real participant was brought in to do an experiment, and there was another 'participant' there (actually a fake) who was doing a learning task. A rationale or story was provided for shocking the 'participant' who was 'learning'; the real participant had to give an electric shock to the other if they got a learning problem wrong. Notice already that this depends on the experimenter convincing the real participant of this story. Notice again also, that there were no alternative behaviours possible—only shock the 'learner' or stop the experiment. But any real participant going against the experimenter's instructions to stop the experiment *would need to provide a counter story or narrative*.

So, we need to look at the whole context, and most of the points made elsewhere also apply here. The participants were strangers, and the results found probably would never have happened if friends, family, or kin-based communities were used. This was done within a Western institution with hierarchies and ongoing status displays, especially for the experimenters. Like the original 'cognitive dissonance' experiments, so much depends on how well the experimenter presents the fake story. But with no alternative behaviours (or easy exit) possible for the participants (unlike like real life), there was not much they could do otherwise. Some of these contexts were shown when Milgram varied some 'factors'.

The results were found in context, there is no disputing that much. But the point that has been made numerous times is that these were mostly very specific contexts that would hardly apply in the real world. The analogy is often made to those who obey an authoritarian or harsh regime, but in such cases they are acting under a very different and strong context of being punished if they fail to obey—not really comparable. This would require a Milgram scenario in which the participants were told that if they did not obey the instructions given by the experimenter they would be severely punished or shot. A very different context, so the fact that Milgram got compliance with instruction cannot then 'explain' real-world examples of *why* people obey. As always, to do that we must observe over time for the *specific contexts* and no amount of experimental variations will cover all these. So, 'explaining' real-world obedience by saying that it is the 'Milgram effect' is a very poor and simplistic 'explanation'.

Bystander intervention, social loafing, social facilitation, deindividuation, and social competition

These are treated as nominalized unique social 'phenomena' within social psychology, but they are just ways of varying social consequences from strangers (see earlier in the chapter for the ten common consequences used in social psychology experiments) that have been measured in different ways (Guerin, 1999, 2003). These are not distinct phenomena, therefore, but *different arrangements of general social outcomes from strangers* that might impact on participants in experiments. This discursive reasoning strategy, used here by social psychologists, is really about the synthesis of structure and function (see Chapter 2). If a situation is made repetitive (controlled in experiments) then the result will look like a 'thing' or 'object' structure; but you can vary this so the functioning can be seen and not a permanent 'phenomenon'.

Table 9.2 outlines how the differences found in the research literature are only in how they were administered and what the contexts were.

Of course, all these experimental settings got rid of all normal context in which these named 'phenomena' might occur. If friends, family, or kin-based groups were used in similar experiments, instead of strangers, the results would be very different. These effects only work as found in stranger or contractual social relationships. These names are not unique 'phenomena' of social life.

Table 9.2 Six 'phenomena' from social psychology and how they differ only because they use different manipulations of social consequences and different measurements

'Unique' social psychological phenomenon	Experimental manipulation of social consequences	What was the measure?
Bystander intervention	Anonymity (no monitoring possible) through being in small or large groups	Helping behaviours of many sorts
Social loafing	Anonymity and evaluation	Productive output
Deindividuation	Anonymity was reduced in several ways	'Deviant' or 'anti-normative' behaviours
Social facilitation	A stranger was present or not (hence anonymity and no monitoring)	Productive output (and other behaviours)
Social competition (Guerin, 2003)	Being in small or large groups	Productive output and anti-normative behaviours
Modified social loafing (Guerin, 1999)	Alone or in groups, and identifiable or not	Productive output and anti-normative behaviours

References

Allport, F. H. (1924). *Social psychology*. Boston, MA: Houghton Mifflin.
Armistead, N. (Ed.) (1974). *Reconstructing social psychology*. Harmondsworth, UK: Penguin.
Cartwright, D., & Zander, A. (1953). *Group dynamics: Research and theory*. New York, NY: Harper & Row.
Doise, W. (1986). *Levels of explanation in social psychology*. Cambridge, UK: Cambridge University Press.
Douglas, M. (Ed.) (1973). *Rules & meanings: The anthropology of everyday knowledge*. London: Penguin.
Edwards, D. (1997). *Discourse and cognition*. London: Sage.
Edwards, D., & Potter, J. (1992). *Discursive psychology*. London: Sage.
Edwards, D., & Potter, J. (1993). Language and causation: A discursive action model of description and attribution. *Psychological Review, 100*, 23–41.
Festinger, L. (1957). *A theory of cognitive dissonance*. Stanford, CA: Stanford University Press.
Festinger, L., & Carlsmith, J. M. (1959). Cognitive consequences of forced compliance. *Journal of Abnormal and Social Psychology, 58*, 203–210.
Fishbein, M., & Ajzen, I. (1975). *Belief, attitude, intention, and behavior: An introduction to theory and research*. Reading, MA: Addison-Wesley.
Fiske, S., & Taylor, S. E. (1984). *Social cognition*. New York, NY: McGraw-Hill.
Gough, B., McFadden, M., & McDonald, M. (2013). *Critical social psychology: An introduction*. New York, NY: Red Globe Press.
Guerin, B. (1991). Anticipating the consequences of social behavior. *Current Psychology: Research and Reviews, 10*, 131–162.
Guerin, B. (1993). *Social facilitation*. Cambridge, UK: Cambridge University Press.
Guerin, B. (1994). Attitudes and beliefs as verbal behavior. *Behavior Analyst, 17*, 155–163.
Guerin, B. (1999). Social behaviors as determined by different arrangements of social consequences: Social loafing, social facilitation, deindividuation, and a modified social loafing. *Psychological Record, 49*, 565–578.
Guerin, B. (2001a). Individuals as social relationships: 18 ways that acting alone can be thought of as social behavior. *Review of General Psychology, 5*, 406–428.
Guerin, B. (2001b). Replacing catharsis and uncertainty reduction theories with descriptions of the historical and social context. *Review of General Psychology, 5*, 44–61.
Guerin, B. (2003). Social behaviors as determined by different arrangements of social consequences: Diffusion of responsibility effects with competition. *Journal of Social Psychology, 143*, 313–329.
Guerin, B. (2016). *How to rethink psychology: New metaphors for understanding people and their behavior*. London: Routledge.
Guerin, B. (2018). The use of participatory and non-experimental research methods in behavior analysis. *Revista Perspectivas em Anályse Comportamento, 9*, 248–264.

Guerin, B., Leugi, G. B., & Thain, A. (2018). Attempting to overcome problems shared by both qualitative and quantitative methodologies: Two hybrid procedures to encourage diverse research. *Australian Community Psychologist, 29*, 74–90.

Harré, R., & Secord, P. F. (1972). *The explanation of social behaviour*. London: Blackwell.

Lana, R. E. (1991). *Assumptions of social psychology: A re-examination*. Hillsdale, NJ: Erlbam.

Milgram, S. (1974). *Obedience to authority: An experimental view*. New York, NY: Harper & Row.

Mills, C. W. (1940). Situated actions and vocabularies of motive. *American Sociological Review, 5*, 904–913.

Moscovici, S. (1961/2008). *Psychoanalysis. Its image, its public*. London: Polity Press.

Murphy, G., Murphy, L. B., & Newcomb, T. M. (1931). *Experimental social psychology: An interpretation of research upon the socialization of the individual*. London: Harper & Brothers.

Potter, J. (1996). *Representing reality: Discourse, rhetoric and social construction*. London: Sage.

Potter, J., & Edwards, D. (1990). Nigel Lawson's tent: Discourse analysis, attribution theory and the social psychology of fact. *European Journal of Social Psychology, 20*, 405–424.

Potter, J., Wetherell, M., & Chitty, A. (1991). Quantification rhetoric: Cancer on television. *Discourse & Society, 2*, 333–365.

Putcha, C., & Potter, J. (2002). Manufacturing individual opinions: Market research focus groups and the discursive psychology of evaluation. *British Journal of Social Psychology, 41*, 435–363.

Shaw, M. E., & Constanzo, P. R. (1970). *Theories of social psychology*. London: McGraw-Hill.

Siedentop, L. (2004). *Inventing the individual: The origins of Western liberalism*. London: Penguin.

Skinner, B. F. (1957). *Verbal behavior*. Englewood Cliffs, NJ: Prentice Hall.

Tajfel, H. (Ed.) (1984). *The social dimension*. Volume 1. Cambridge, UK: Cambridge University Press.

Thomas, W. I., & Thomas, D. S. (1928). *The child in America: Behavior problems and programs*. New York, NY: Knopf.

Tuffin, K. (2004). *Understanding critical social psychology*. London: Sage.

Wetherell, M., & Potter, J. (1992). *Mapping the language of racism: Discourse and the legitimation of exploitation*. London: Harvester Wheatsheaf.

Index

Note: Page numbers in **bold** refer to tables.

abstractions 7, 109, 112, 152
agreement: and the arts 124; and beliefs 78, 80, 85–87; Marxism 108; rationality and 2, 4, 16, 17, 30
Allport, F. H. 146, 147
ambiguity 125, 135–136, 138
ancient Greece and Rome 1–3, 7
animisms 139
anthropology *see* social anthropology
Aristotle 102
the arts 119–125
attitudes 76, **156**, 160, 161
attribution 18, 19, 29, 101–102, 120, 128, 132
attribution biases 161

Beattie, J. H. M. 29
Beck, U. 73–74
behaviour analysis 37–38
beliefs 161; contradictory 158–159; emotional 88, 125; and language strategies 76–88; rationality and 84, 119; *see also* religion
biases *see* cognitive biases
Blacking, J. 76, 123
Bleuler, E. 91–92
bonding: and the arts 124; and beliefs 29, 81, 86, 87; social relationships **68**
Bottomore, T. 116
bullying: and the arts 123, 124; beliefs and 85–86; bureaucracies and **72**; capitalism and **69**; rationality and 2

bureaucracy: capitalism and **70–72**, 73; historical 53; neoliberalism and **13**, 59, 60, 61; rationality and **12**, 19, 25–26; rituals and 9, 138; secrecy and **63**; and social relationships 8
bystander intervention **163**

capitalism: beliefs and 80, 84, 85; identity and 94; Marxism and 107, 111, 116; rationality and 5–7, 10, 16, 19, 20; social relationships and 50, 52, 55, 57, 58, 60, **68–69**, **70–72**, 73, 74; social structures and 45
Carlsmith, J. M. 159
Catholic Church 128, 138
Child, A. B. 129
Child, I. L. 129
China 53, 77
Chomsky, N. 39, 43, 44
Christianity 28; *see also* Catholic Church
class 36, 41, 45, 104, 116, 152
cognitive biases 158
cognitive dissonance 81, 158–160
colonization 55, 59
community, size of 6
competition: and the arts 123, 124; and beliefs 85–86; economics and 20; social relationships and **66**, **68**, **163**
complaining: and the arts 124; and beliefs 87; social relationships and 54
compliance 134, 159, 162

conflict: and the arts 125; and beliefs 81, 87; bureaucracy and 61; social relationships and 56, 74, 81, 108, 114
consciousness 95–100, 110, 111–116, 146
consequences: Marxism and 113–116; rationality and 1, 3–5, 8, 10, 15, 17–19, 22–25, 29; religion 131, 132, 134, 135, 138; social relationships and 43, 57, **64**, **68**, **70**, 99, 147, 148, 149–151, **163**
contractual relationships *see* stranger relationships
contradictions 107–108, 114
control: and the arts 124–125; behaviours and 99–100; and beliefs 87; of populations 80, 83, 136; personality and 44; strangers and 58
cooperation: and the arts 124; and beliefs 78, 86; rationality and 26; and religion 131, 134, 138; resources and 51, 53
cults 82
cultural practices 51

deindividuation **163**
Deleuze, G. 108, 109
Delphi, Temple of 102
Diagnostic and Statistical Manual of Mental Disorders see DSM
dialectic 2, 3, 4, 106–109, 114
Dialogues of Plato 1–2
Dianetics 139
distancing: and the arts 124; and beliefs 86
domestic violence 85, 134
Drucker, P. 21
DSM (*Diagnostic and Statistical Manual of Mental Disorders*) 10, **12**, 19
DuBois, C. 21
Durkheim, E. 40, 132, 133, 145

ecology **13**, 26–28
economics: identity and 92; Marxism and 106; rationality and **12**, 20–23, 26; social relationships and 49–50, 52–53, 60
ego 89

Engels, F. 105–106, 109, 112
Enlightenment 5, 28
Esterson, A. 19
Evans-Pritchard, E. E. 25, 134, 136, 137

faith *see* religion
family relationships 6, **27**, **62–67**
Festinger, L. 159
Firth, R. 39
food 20–22, 42, 49, 55, 57, 129, 131–132
forced compliance paradigm 159
Fortes, M. 134
France 22
Freud, S. 89, 129–130
Freudianism 48
friendships **27**, 28, 56, **62–67**, 86, 87

Galileo 17
Geertz, C. 137–138
Gellner, E. 17
gender 43, 45, 46, 58–59; *see also* patriarchy
generalization 7
Gestalt theory 89, 127, 144, 154; triangle sensory experiment 148
Gibson, J. J.149, 154
Gifford, E. W. 21
Gluckman, M. 25, 137
Goode, P. 116
government: beliefs and 80, 87; Marxism and 107; rationality and **13**, 22, 25–26; social relationships and 60, 61, **64**, **70**, **71**
grammar 39, 43–44, 115, 121, 123
Guerin, B. 40, 72
Gumplowicz, L. 37, 38–39
Gurvitch, G. 106

Halliday, M. 39
Hamilton, M. B. 130
Hargrove, B. 129
hedging: and the arts 124; and beliefs 79, 87; Marxism 113
Hegel, G. 106
'historical materialism' 106
humbling: and the arts 125; and beliefs 88
Hume, D. 152

Humeanism 146
humour: and the arts 125; and beliefs 80, 87–88; and bureaucracies **72**
hunter gatherers 52, 53

idealism 105, 110, 111, 114
identity 89–102; kin-based communities and 92–93; Marxism and 109; in modernity 93–95; religion and 130; self-awareness and 95–100; social relationships and **65**, **69**, **72**; social structures and 35, 161
image management: and the arts 124; and beliefs 86, 88; social relationships and **66**
Indigenous peoples 16–17, 20, 21–22, 24–26, 28, 134, 136
individualism 16, 38, 73, 74, 90, 145–147, 153
isolation 82

James, W. 127

Kafka, F. 9
Keen, I. 135
kin-based relationships: beliefs and 84; identity and 90–91, 92–93, 94; Marxism and 105; and natural environment **27**; rationality and 19, 24, **27**, 29; social relationships 56, **62–67**
Kroeber, A. L. 21

Laing, R. D. 19
language: abstractions and 152; the arts and 120–123; beliefs and 76–88; bureaucracy and 61; consequences and 121; grammar 39, 43–44, 115, 121, 123; identity and 89, 90, 96, 98; Marxism and 104, 105, 107–109, 111, 112–113, 115–116; rationality and 4–5, 7, 8, **12**, **14**, 18, 155; social relationships and 51, 61, **64**, **67**, 148, 153; *see also* linguistics
law and legal systems **13**, 23–25, 58
Lenin, V. 106, 107, 108
Lévi-Strauss, C. 136
Lewis, N. 28
linguistics 39, 41, 43–44

logic 1–3, 5–7, **12**, **14**, 21, 26, 30; beliefs and 81; Marxism and 106, 108–109

Maine, H. 24
Mao Zedong 106, 108
Marwick, M. G. 29
Marx, K. 56, 105–106, 107, 108, 109–112, 115–117
Marxism 104–117; class structures 46, 104, 116; social relations of production 105–106
mental health **12**, 17, 18–20, 72, 74, 76, 83, 139
metaphysics 110, 112, 114–115
Milgram, S. 162
modernity Beck on 73–74; bureaucracy and 25, 59, 61; environment and 28; rationality and 19; self in 91, 92, 93–95; social relationships and 53–55
monetary relationships *see* stranger relationships
money: beliefs 80; *forced compliance* and 159; rationality and 3, 5–7, 8, 10, 11, **12**, 20–23, 28; social relationships and 55, 57, 58, 59, **62**, **63**, **66**, **68–69**, **70**, 73
Moscovici, S. 145
Munro, D. J. 77

natural environment *see* ecology
neoliberalism: rationality and 11, **12**, **13**, 19, 26; social relationships and 59, 60, 61, **68–69**, 73–74
Nietzsche, F. 30, 108, 109
non-rational persuasion 9–30; ecology and 26–28; economics and 20–23; government and bureaucracy 25–26; law and legal systems 23–25; logic and 30; mental health and 18–20; religion and spirituality and 28–29; science and 11, 15–18

obedience 162
opportunity structured systems 58

Pathway 1 143–144, 147, 148, 151, 154, 159, 161; beliefs and 77, 84; identity and 101; individualism

and 36, 37; Marxism and 110–111; neuroscience and 48; rationality and 15; religion and 127–128, 129–130, 131–135, 139; social relationships and 73
Pathway 2 154–155; Marxism and 110, 111, 116; religion and 128, 130–131, 134–135, 137, 139
patriarchy 42, 45, 58–59
personal crises 135
personality 44–45, 144
'personality variables' 152
persuasion 1–5, 7, 9, 10, **14**, **65**, 108–109
Plato 1–2
Plekhanov, G. 108, 109
policing 58, **64**, **70**
politeness: and the arts 125; and beliefs 79, 87; and bureaucracies **72**; and capitalism **69**; social relationships and 27, **65**
population size 7, 52, 53, 54, 55, 56, 57–59
Powdermaker, H. 21
predictive behaviour patterns 41
'primitive' societies **13**, 16, 17, 20, 21, 24, 26, 134
production, social relations of 105–106
protection: and the arts 124; and beliefs 87
psychology, 1960s **14**
public opinion 23

Radcliffe-Brown, A. R. 132–133
rationality 1–30; beliefs and 84, 119; bureaucracy and 19, 25–26; capitalism and 5–7, 10, 16, 19, 20; economics and **12**, 20–23, 26; emotions 152; government and **13**, 22, 25–26; individualism and 146; kin-based communities and 19, 24, **27**, 29; language and 4–5, 7, 8, **12**, **14**, 18, 155; modernity and 19; money and 3, 5–7, 8, 10, 11, **12**, 20–23, 28; neoliberalism and 11, **12**, **13**, 19, 26; resource production and distribution and **12–13**, 23; science and 5, 7–10, 11, **12**, 15–18, 28–29; sharing and **12**, 21

reciprocating: and the arts 124; and beliefs 86
religion 127–139; bonding 81; cooperation and 131, 134, 138; functions of 129–131; identity and 130; rationality and **12**, 28–29; social anthropology and 128–129, 131, 132, 136; social control and 80, 131–136; sociology and 128, 129, 132, 143, 145; *see also* Catholic Church; Christianity; Indigenous peoples; rituals
research methodologies as social relationships 154–157
resource production and distribution 43; identity and 92; Marxism and 105; rationality and **12–13**, 23; social relationships and 49–53, 54, 55, 57–58, 60, 73
resource–social relationship pathways: the arts and 121, 122, 124; beliefs and 84–86, 87; identity and 90, 93; Marxism and 105–106, 107, 116; religion and 130; social relationships and 50–55, 57, 58, **62**
rhetoric 2–4, 161
Riches, D. 130, 132, 134
rituals: and the arts 120; rationality and 9, **13**, 16, 27, 29; religion and 129, 131–135, 137–138; social relationships and **64**; social structures and 45, 53
rudeness: and the arts 125; and beliefs 87

Sahlins, M. 21
'schizophrenia' 91
science and rationality 5, 7–10, 11, **12**, 15–18, 28–29
Scientology 139
self-awareness 95–100
shamanism 136
sharing: and the arts 124; and beliefs 81, 86; and rationality **12**, 21; social relationships and 52, **62**
showing off: and the arts 125; and beliefs 88
Sibelius, J. 122
Skinner, B. F. 38, 39, 148, 154
Smith, A. 20

social anthropology 43, 45, 154; identity and 92; Marxism and 105; religion and 128–129, 131, 132, 136; social relationships and 48, 49, 50, 52–53, 56
social competition **163**
social contextual analyses 38, 104–105, 111, 117
'social dissonance' 81, 158
social facilitation **163**
social loafing **163**
social psychology 143–163; assumptions of 145–155
social relationships 48–74; bureaucratic neoliberalism and 60, 61, **70–72**; individual behaviour and 37–39, 42–43; modernity and 53–55; societal systems 35–46
sociology 153, 154; beliefs and 84; individualism and 37–39, 42–43; rationality and 6; religion and 128, 129, 132, 143, 145
Socrates 2
Spencer, R. F. 22
stranger (contractual) relationships: and the arts 120; beliefs and 85; identity and 94; Marxism and 105; and natural environment **27**; rationality and 6, 11, **13**, 19, 20, 24, 25, 26, **27**, 28, 29; social relationships and 55, 57, 58, 60, 61, **62–69**, 73–74; universality and 153
Suttles, W. 22

taboo 129, 131–132
Thomas, W. I. 145, 147–148, 149
Thomas Aquinas 28
totemism 133–134, 136, 138, 139
triangle sensory experiment 148

urbanization 7

Vygotsky, L. 104, 111

Wallis, R. 128
Wilson, B. R. 138
witchcraft **12**, **13**, 24, 29, 136
Wittgenstein, L. 153
word- or rule-based systems 55
Wundt, W. 37, 42
Wundtian traditions 48